Dangerous Brown Men

Dangerous Brown Men

Exploiting Sex, Violence and Feminism in the War on Terror

GARGI BHATTACHARYYA

Zed Books
LONDON & NEW YORK

Dangerous Brown Men: Exploiting Sex, Violence and Feminism in the War on Terror was first published in 2008 by Zed Books Ltd, 7 Cynthia Street, London N1 9JF, UK and Room 400, 175 Fifth Avenue, New York, NY 10010, USA

www.zedbooks.co.uk

Set in 11/13 pt Granjon and Trebuchet
By Long House Publishing Services
Cover designed by Andrew Corbett
Printed and bound in Malta by Gutenberg Press, Ltd.

Distributed in the USA exclusively by Palgrave Macmillan, 175 Fifth Avenue, New York, NY 10010, USA

A catalogue record for this book is available from the British Library
Library of Congress Cataloging in Publication Data available

ISBN 978 1 84277 878 4 hb
ISBN 978 1 84277 879 1 pb

Contents

Acknowledgements

Thanks to my former colleagues at the University of Birmingham and to my new colleagues at Aston University for support during the completion of this work.

I am grateful to COMPAS (the Centre for Migration Policy and Society), the ESRC seminar series 'Multiculturalism, Ethics and the War on Terror' and MaMSIE (Mapping Maternal Subjectivities, Identities and Ethics) for giving me opportunities to present earlier versions of some of these ideas.

As always, I could not have completed this or anything else without the support of Manju, Dilip, Sonali and Stanheed.

For me, this project began with the birth of Swadhin, my own most special dangerous brown man, who has helped me to remember again that every detainee and torture victim, every terror suspect and media demon, is someone's darling baby. This book is for you, with the hope that by the time you are old enough to read it, this will all seem like ancient history.

Introduction
Dangerous Brown Men?

The War on Terror has brought forth a range of public representations and new documents revealing what is considered necessary in
times of war. These include images and video clips, soundbites and
websites, all seeping into a transnational public consciousness and
creating a highly suggestive montage of what this new conflict is and
what it might mean. The documents stem from many sources, from
both the US and its allies, from declared enemies of the West and
independent sources, and from old and new media outlets. It feels as if
we know lots of snippets of information about this nebulous war, even
if few can construct a comprehensible overall narrative. It is impossible for the consumer of such global media to be unaware that
horrors are being carried out 'in our name'.

We know, for example, that many many people have been detained
without charge or trial at Guantánamo and other less high-profile
detention facilities. We know that these detainees include children.
We know that some of those detained have sustained permanent
injury – losing the sight of eyes, pieces of feet, arms – although we do
not know how such injuries came about. We know, from video images
– taken through the fence at Guantánamo – of emaciated men being
manhandled by guards, that people are kept almost naked. We know
that others at Guantánamo and elsewhere are being stripped naked as
a softening-up tactic in interrogation. We know that detainees attempt
to protest by hunger strike and are force-fed in brutal and possibly
illegal ways. We know that detainees have suffered torture, including
waterboarding, electric shocks and sexual assault. We know that
people have been kidnapped and flown secretly to places where they
have been handed to torturers, incarcerated in the living death of
secret prisons. We know that some have died. We know that some

1

have been beaten and raped and abused, apparently for the enjoyment of their guards. We know that they have been repeatedly cut on their genitals, that these cuts caused permanent scarring.

All of this, which is not a secret and which is not denied by the perpetrators, is presented as justified in the struggle against 'bad men', as George Bush has described those imprisoned at Guantánamo Bay (Stafford Smith, 2007).

My argument is that this presentation of the necessity of brutality in a global war against a non-state enemy, 'international terrorism', is serving to create a new form of global audience and consciousness. The War on Terror, as its proponents term it, is causing a cultural shift in how we are able to conceive of a linked global public and what constitutes membership, even reluctant membership, of such a sphere.

It also represents the attempted creation of a global public space of alliance against terrorism. I want to suggest that the development of this global arena – however contested – is a central aspect of the War on Terror. Of course, in some ways this is obviously the case. We know only too well that the battle is between 'us' and 'them', that it is a battle of cultures and values, that what is under attack is 'our very way of life'. Sometimes it seems that the primary justification presented for this war is that of culture (Northcott, 2004; Gow, 2004; Drury, 2006).

This work is necessarily about the representations of the War on Terror in and through the UK and US – although it attempts to describe the construction of a global public that goes beyond these central players in the 'coalition of the willing'. The underlying argument is that the War on Terror combines a reclaiming of dirty warfare as a necessary evil in the defence of democracy (or 'our way of life' etc.), an attempted rewriting of the proper jurisdiction of international law (with implications for the terms of consensus around legality within national spaces), and an aspiration to create a global audience and polity that participates in 'our' way of life.

It is not suggested that readings of the images and documents that represent the War on Terror to a wider public reveal the ideological intentions behind this conflict. Future scholars with access to a wider range of documentation may uncover explicit plans for the conduct of culture wars, just as scholars of the Cold War have revealed the extent and range of cultural organs involved in that other global conflict (Stonor Saunders, 1999). Neither is it argued that any such attempts to deploy cultural artefacts for political gain are marred by secrecy. The War on Terror has raised far more troubling moral questions than whether it is honest to use cultural products to attempt to shape public opinion.

Instead this work attempts to identify the manner in which these widely circulated and not-denied texts reposition those who see them as participants in this new global public. Whatever the intention, this has been one of the effects of the War on Terror and it is an effect created through an insistent repetition of ideas about bodies and sexuality, gender and race and entitlement, values and progress and violence.

In common with many others, I am beginning from my own sense of fear and bewilderment. Something has changed with the so-called War on Terror, however much this builds on previous strategies of state racism and human rights abuse, of overt and covert occupation, of nurturing authoritarian regimes as allies in the battle to safeguard 'our' interests, whether identified as geopolitical, economic or cultural in some more nebulous sense.

I know full well that this is not the first time of horror. Our era has no monopoly on abuse and violence. Perhaps nothing that is happening has not happened before. Probably much of the activity of the War on Terror is a continuation of previous state activity, be that overt or covert (for some infamous examples see Huggins, 1991; Dillon, 1991; MacMaster, 2002). Yet there is something if not new at least unfamiliar about the presentation and processes of the War on Terror. Not least there is the continual reaffirmation by its proponents that this is indeed a completely new era, a time when the new and irrepressible demons of international terrorism are such that we can no longer afford the indulgences of previous times. International law, the protection of human rights and civil liberties, the right to a fair trial – now we are told that these things are not necessarily absolutes. Each one is negotiable, subject to flexibility and perhaps altogether expendable because the battle to defeat terrorism requires that we sacrifice such niceties (most famously outlined by Dershowitz, 2002, with the larger debate summarised in many sources, including Bufacchi and Arrigo, 2006; Greenberg, 2006; Ramsey, 2006; Foot, 2006).

This then is the first element – the retreat from previously accepted standards of international conduct in conflict. It is not suggested that such standards have been respected at all times. What is new is the continual assertion that these rules of engagement no longer apply. One aspect of this work examines the manner and content of such assertions in order to understand their role in the attempted creation of a global public space.

This is the second element of the work. The War on Terror is not only a series of military interventions and transnational security measures; it also entails a cultural project that seeks to remake the terms of belonging, legality and otherness (Mahajan, 2002). This is truly a project of the globalised era, highly mediatised, revealing the emergence of new and shifting relationships between regions, nations and communities. The public narrative of the War on Terror describes a world where old histories of geopolitical alliance can alter course in a moment, a world where all can join the righteous battle against terrorism.

The central contention of this work is that this cultural project operates through the deployment of ideas of sexuality and race. I am trying here to bring together information from a range of sources, from factual material by other researchers to public pronouncements by key actors to more creative engagements with the War on Terror. In the process I hope both to present an analysis of the impact of these cultural texts and their circulation and to represent something of the panic-ridden sensibility of our age.

This is not an attempt to uncover what has been kept secret. I have relied heavily on other authors and publicly available documents in order to outline the activities of the War on Terror. What I am seeking to add to this debate is an examination of how this knowledge circulates in public life. A battle about the terms of legality, anti-terrorism and the rights of the individual is being carried out through the global media. Representations of the War on Terror, both of what such a project entails and of why such actions may be necessary, form an integral part of this cultural battle.

Feminism and the war

Feminist scholars have drawn attention to the place of sexualisation and racism in the workings of new imperial forces. Chandra Mohanty summarises this concern and reiterates the need for a feminist response:

imperialism, militarization, and globalization all traffic in women's bodies, women's labor, and ideologies of masculinity/femininity, heteronormativity, racism, and nationalism to consolidate and reproduce power and domination. Thus, it is anti-racist, anti-imperialist, anti-capitalist, multiply gendered feminist praxis that can provide the ground for dismantling empire and re-envisioning just, humane and secure home-spaces for marginalized communities globally. (Mohanty, 2006, 9)

In many ways my project here is an expansion of this paragraph. I have tried to trace the manner in which women's bodies are represented and circulated in order to examine the particular formations of gender, sexuality, race and nation that are brought into play in the War on Terror. However, unlike Mohanty and others, I am less certain that such ideologies of gender and sexuality, or of race and nation, easily replay our expectations of what is normative, dominant and rewarded. This work argues that the War on Terror combines painfully familiar forms of violence and exclusion with a rhetorical embrace of gender equality, multicultural coexistence and personal liberty that reveals the imprint of more recent influences.

We argued that postcolonial and advanced capitalist states had specific features in common. They own the means of organized violence, which is often deployed in the service of national security. Thus, for instance, the USA Patriot Act is mirrored by similar post-9/11 laws in Japan and India. Second, the militarization of postcolonial and advanced capitalist states essentially means the re-masculinization of the state apparatus, and of daily life. Third, nation-states invent and solidify practices of racialization and sexualization of their peoples, disciplining and mobilizing the bodies of women, especially poor and third world women, as a way of consolidating patriarchal and colonizing processes. Thus the transformation of 'private' to 'public' patriarchies in multinational factories, and the rise of the international 'maid trade', the sex tourism industry, global militarized prostitution, and so on. Finally, nation-states deploy heterosexual citizenship through legal and other means. (Mohanty, 2006, 10)

Although I agree with the broad thrust of this outline, this volume argues something slightly different about the characteristics and content of the racialisation and sexualisation of populations. If the militarisation of such advanced states entails a remasculinisation, then the terms of this masculinity are also undergoing significant renegotiation. Similarly, such states may ratchet up 'patriarchal and colonizing processes', but this involves a disciplining of male and female bodies in a manner that combines familiar 'patriarchies' with reworkings of the place and meaning of gendered bodies. This is what Laura Sjoberg describes when she writes the following of the Iraq war:

> The story of the conflict was not only told in terms of American manliness, but in terms of the victory of American manliness over the mistaken and inferior masculinities of the Iraqi opponent. ... American masculinity (courage, benevolence and self-sacrifice) was better than Iraqi masculinity (defiance, lunacy and random violence). This sense of superiority of American masculinity may have created social space to allow the occurrence of the torture, which feminized the inferior masculinity. (Sjoberg, 2007, 95)

The cultural reference points of the War on Terror are shaped by the cultural politics of recent years. The key components of the justificatory narrative surrounding the war are taken from progressive social movements – the defence of women's rights, the celebration of more diverse masculinities which can express emotion and enact relations of care, the affirmation of multicultural coexistence and the implication that backward cultures remain entrapped in uncontrollable and excessive homophobia in contrast to our tolerance within careful confines. The proclamation of openness and innovation is an important element of how advanced capitalism bills itself in the War on Terror. For this reason, the deployment of a disciplinary sexualisation cannot easily be reduced to ideas of heterosexual citizenship. In an era where enemies of the West are portrayed as lacking the ability to gain pleasure from even the most straightforward of heterosexual relations, western culture is presented as tolerant and attentive to more diverse methods of showing love and experiencing pleasure. The alleged sexual dysfunction that is attributed to extremists and terrorists becomes contrasted with the supposedly healthy attitude to sexuality that characterises free societies (for a fictionalised account of this distinction, see Amis, 2007).

Stuart Croft has collated the myriad ways in which the attacks of 11 September 2001 (9/11) have been deployed as a founding myth of shared consciousness and cultural affiliation (Croft, 2006). Following the attacks there was a very quick, seemingly almost immediate, articulation of a shared narrative of what it meant to belong. Included in this story, a story assembled from many sources, was the sense that our way of life included an attention to the rights of women. The identification of Afghanistan and the Taliban as the harbourers of international terrorism demanded an explanation of how they differed from us. Perhaps for the first time, the need to defend the rights of women was presented among the justifications and objectives of war. In an address in December 2001, George Bush assembled the key components of the narrative that was mobilised to distinguish between 'us' and 'them'.

> This new enemy seeks to destroy our freedom and impose its views. We value life; the terrorists ruthlessly destroy it. We value education; the terrorists do not believe women should be educated or should have health care, or should leave their homes. We value the right to speak our minds; for the terrorists, free expression can be grounds for execution. We respect people of all faiths and welcome the free practice of religion; our enemy wants to dictate how to think and how to worship even to their fellow Muslims. (George Bush, 2001)

Here the associations are spelt out. The new enemy opposes that which we value and respect – freedom, life, education, women's rights, free speech, religious freedom; the inclusion of women's rights extends the repertoire of freedom claims and confirms that, in the context of the War on Terror, women's rights function as a link in an associative chain referencing otherwise somewhat abstracted markers of freedom. For Bush and others, such an inclusion also served as evidence of the civilisational progress achieved beyond the Muslim world.

There were dissenting voices from the start. In October 2001 a group of US-based feminist academics issued a statement entitled 'Transnational Feminist Practices against War'. This short declaration summarises a number of key points that were being debated in anti-war circles, including the role of the US and other affluent nations in a global system of exploitation and violence, the slide between racist foreign policy and state racism against minorities at home, and a critique of any deployment of liberal feminist goals that was not alert to this global context. However, as well as these well-trodden themes, the statement also touches on ideas that are less often articulated in this arena: ideas of sexuality and of affect.

The 'first and foremost' critique is of the 'thoroughly gendered and racialized effects of nationalism':

> the emerging nationalist discourses consist of misleading and highly senti-mentalized narratives that, among other things, reinscribe compulsory

heterosexuality and the rigidly dichotomized gender roles upon which it is based. A number of icons constitute the ideal types in the drama of nationalist domesticity that we see displayed in the mainstream media. These include the masculine citizen-soldier, the patriotic wife and mother, the breadwinning father who is head of household, and the properly reproductive family. (Bacchetta et al., 2001)

This volume seeks to explore the continuing remaking of such sexual myths in the conduct of the War on Terror. Feminists and others have argued that a variety of nationalist discourses display insistent and problematic propagation of gender inequality and sexual violence (Yuval-Davis, 1997). This is the debate to which the statement above appeals, the body of knowledge that has been uncovered through a scholarship that is attentive to the place of gender, sexuality and affective relations in stories of power and politics. The critique of the nationalist discourses that emerged in the aftermath of the attacks of 9/11 builds on these insights. Once again, the attempt to construct a national body that binds people together and silences contradictions and dissent looks to ideal types of masculinity and femininity because these are the stories that resonate with our most personal ideas of self. In the face of terrorist attacks that despise 'our' way of life, our way of life comes to be represented as a familial drama, all idealised gender types and affective relations. Although the statement here identifies a retreat into dreams of normative heterosexuality, with Americanness being signified through the old tropes of mom and dad, I wonder if the appeal has been more to a sense that 'we' feel and they do not. The family drama, then, with all its strong-jawed fighting and working men and doting women, serves as a metaphor for the relations of care that exemplify all that is best in our way of life.

Although they do not quite say this, the signatories to the statement do identify the assumption that Americans hold a monopoly on human feeling as another central and problematic theme in responses to 9/11. Speaking of various initiatives to counsel students about the trauma of the day, they write:

they tended to assume that 9/11 marked the first time Americans experienced vulnerability, overlooking not only the recent events of the Oklahoma City federal building bombing, but moreover erasing the personal experiences of many immigrants and US people of color for whom 'America' has been a site of potential or realized violence for all of their lives. (Bacchetta et al., 2001)

The linking theme through these ideas is that 9/11 triggered a reinvigoration of American nationalism and, for this reason, the critique is of this re-emergent and triumphalist nationalism. Of course, it is true that there has been a discernible reclaiming of the most overt jingoism and it seems clear that US domestic politics remains highly susceptible to the call of nationalism. However, the rhetoric of the War on Terror is addressed to an audience beyond the confines of the US. This is a global project of cultural and political reconstruction. There are important elements of reinscribing and reinforcing Americanness but there is also an appeal to an emerging global public. This is made explicit in some of the key pronouncements of the War on Terror: 'with us or against us' defines a political and cultural boundary not a national one; the so-called Axis of Evil represents, supposedly, a transnational alliance built on antipathy to shared cultural values of democratic nations or, perhaps more accurately, nations that accept the unassailable power of transnational capital and aspire to the consumer freedoms that it promises.

This volume is interested in the cultural work involved in the creation of the War on Terror alliance. It is an alliance that has no formal existence – this is not a new NATO, or at least not yet. Instead this grouping is linked tenuously through an appeal to shared values, through that most nebulous of ties, culture. And as with all cultural alliances, it can exist only through constant reaffirmation of key myths and narratives. Ideas about gender identity, sexuality and affective relations play a central role in this process, and in the pages that follow I have tried to unpack the workings of such terms in our context of global war.

Sexuality, affect and clashing values

> There is no dividing line – there is a dividing line in our world, not between nations, and not between religions or cultures, but a dividing line separating two visions of justice and the value of life. (George Bush, March 2004)

There are a number of central themes in the particular sexualised racism of the War on Terror. One is the allegation that sex is the particular and defining hang-up of Islam, with this standing in opposition to the supposed sexual liberalism of secular societies. In a number of tellings, Islam is seen to be hung-up about sex, because it is, allegedly, hung-up about women, with the implication that this is proof that it is hung-up about masculinity (for an example of this see Kasem, 2003). Challenging the supposed sexual hang-ups of Islam folds, therefore, into a larger narrative about feminism and women's rights.

As the achievement of rights of a sort for women has become increasingly regarded as a central goal of development, in economic and social terms, the scrutiny of places that do not appear to fulfil these aspirations has increased. The participation of women in public life has become a measure of societal development (see for example the formulation of the Convention for the Elimination of All Forms of Discrimination Against Women). The numbers of under-employed young men in a society has been identified as a future threat to be monitored (Kontominas, 2007; Walker, 2006). The gendering of public life has come to be understood as an important component in our understanding of political movements, violence and extremism.

In relation to the uneven attempts to comprehend developments in the Islamic world, these insights have been reworked by others to argue that the position of Muslim women indicates that contemporary Islam suffers a systematic and deep disturbance about masculinity. This is a mythology that ties debates about the status of women to accusations of intrinsic homophobia and other sexual repression, with all of these indicating a larger dysfunction. However, the psychologised allegation of sexual anxiety leading to sexual and social dysfunction also slides into a different demonisation – that of a sexualised conception of an enemy threat.

Multiculturalism and backlash

A key element of War on Terror discourse is the contention that cultural differences between groups are solid and unchanging and the source of potentially violent conflict. Although Bush, Blair and other central characters have made a point of repeatedly stating the values of tolerance and coexistence as a distinguishing feature of 'our' way of life – and as a crucial differentiation between us and them – the philosophical underpinnings of the War on Terror are shaped by a denial of the possibility of peaceful pluralism. The role of Hunting-ton's conception of the clash of civilisations has been overplayed and his larger vision of a world divided into competing cultural tribes has not been taken up by others (Huntington, 1996). However, his suggestion that discrete cultural types inhabit different geographical areas of the world and that these types are in competition with each other has seeped into political debates within so-called western nations and in the international realm. Coexistence with difference now appears to be impossible – how foolish of us ever to imagine that such a thing could be safe or desirable (Gow, 2004; for an overview of recent debates about multiculturalism see Phillips, 2007; Modood, 2007).

In fact, despite the extensive coverage granted to refutations of multiculturalism and exposures of its failures and limitations, relatively few places have operated explicit policies of multiculturalism at the level of national policy. Key elements of theories of multiculturalism, such as the contention that recognition and respect for cultural identities are necessary for social participation and justice and that appreciation for the contribution of different cultural traditions is a social good, have entered mainstream thinking across many locations. However, such tacit agreements about the benefits of tolerance and coexistence have rarely been formalised into binding policy or legal requirement. Instead, multiculturalism has remained a loosely formulated collection of ideas and recommendations for governing social relations, and includes contradictory elements that are not easily identified as one binding injunction.

Although some of the debates around multiculturalism can appear parochial and focused on the most local and transitory of battles, the question of multiculturalism or something very like it also animates debates about the War on Terror. The ongoing crisis around the possibility of cosmopolitanism or multiculturalism or other conceptions of living with diversity spreads to influence questions about the possibility of international law and workable diplomacy. The two varieties of crisis-talk serve to discredit existing models of conflict avoidance and resolution. Multiculturalism, whatever its shortcomings, attempts to imagine a world that can encompass different identities and ways of being in a manner that respects and values all. If this aspiration is derided as impossible and/or wrong-headed and dangerous, then the small niceties of making space for other kinds of people, in understanding and in practice, no longer make sense. Similarly, if international law and diplomacy have relied on reciprocity between states capable of exercising sovereignty, then such constraints on behaviour between states make no sense in relation to entities that cannot or will not meet the responsibilities of statehood (Cooper, 2004; Rotberg, 2003).

Although these two sets of arguments are not related in any explicit manner, they operate to reinforce each other, and elements of each can be discerned in discussions of the other. The cultural project of the War on Terror, that is the representations and narratives that accompany and legitimise the military actions and the wider attempt to rewrite the terms of law and citizenship within nations, rarely references issues of race directly. However, these two refutations – of multiculturalism and of international law – suffuse the discourse of the War on Terror. In both instances, the underlying suggestion is that there are absolute and impassable differences between cultures and if progressive western values are to be preserved then alien threats must be ruthlessly contained.

Dangerous brown men – is the War on Terror really about sex?

This book argues that the War on Terror is a deeply sexualised endeavour. By this, it is not suggested that this whole global experience is in fact a symptom of sexual frustration or dysfunction or that international relations are motored by deep and primal passions or that all forms of conflict can be reduced to the expression of sexual anxiety. Instead it is argued that there is something deeply and troublingly sexualised about the representation and conduct of the War on Terror and that this sexualisation tells us something about the racialisation of contemporary international relations.

Zillah Eisenstein describes this in terms of sexual decoys – the deployment of highly visible figures in order to give a misleading impression of equality and progress. Eisenstein describes this as increasing the complexity of gender and sexuality: 'There is female and male masculinity; and male and female femininity' (Eisenstein, 2007, xii).

Eisenstein is concerned primarily with the dissonance between the claim to defend women's rights and the practice of what she terms 'US-led anti-democratic wars of/against terror'. However she too suggests that notions of sexuality are doing some extra work in the cultural expressions of the War on Terror. Eisenstein argues that sexual torture and humiliation are inflicted on brown/Muslim men by white women in order to make these men vulnerable like women and to reassert the fiction that women in the West are free, including free to participate in the degradation of racially othered men (Eisenstein, 2007, 34). Implicit in these scenarios is the idea that sexual torture is a source of particular humiliation and un-manning for Muslims and that sexual freedoms are a particular treasure of the West.

Accounts of the history of sexuality explicate this distinction – from the influential writings of Foucault on the medicalisation and excessive production of modern western sexual cultures to the discussion of sexology and its impact on popular consciousness. Sexual liberation is conceived as freedom within the separate sphere of sexuality and intimacy and this separation enables the commodification of sexual expression. I want to suggest that, while we may dispute the western provenance of such a phenomenon, the idea of sex as a space apart from other parts of life seeps into the cultural presentation and conduct of the War on Terror. Writing of the historical construction of sex and pleasure in the West, Gail Hawkes writes of more recent commodifications of sexuality:

> Sex sells, sex retains the power to fascinate and entice, even in an experience-weary world. The assumption that sex is the pleasure of pleasures perpetuates its 'specialness', while at the same time its integration into a world of commodities renders this quality 'mundane'. In both, the long-standing negative constructions that emphasized that sexual pleasure was socially disruptive appear to have been eclipsed. ... whimsical experience of commodified pleasures is not now a problem for social order but operates as one of its foundations. (Hawkes, 2004, 180)

Hawkes is writing of a longer historical process through which the meanings allocated to sex and pleasure have been contested and adapted. However, her account of our time resonates with some key claims from the War on Terror. The simultaneous placing of sexual experience as special, apart and free and as the most everyday aspect of consumer practice echoes the associative links made between sex, rights and the market and the implication that this most free and special of places can be reached through market participation.

In relation to these ideas, this work goes on to explore a number of key themes:

- the contention that sexual freedom is one of the freedoms that 'we' are defending, allegedly, against the intolerance and authoritarianism of violent others;

- that freedom of sexual expression can stand in as an archetypal social 'freedom' because we live in a culture that imagines fulfilment in terms of intimacy and sexual autonomy and views sexual expression as one of the purest expressions of self – what we really really want;

- that at the same time, the conduct of the War on Terror reveals some highly sexualised violence and representations of the 'enemy';

- that the representation of terrorist threat suggests a sexual motivation that underlies the violence of cultural difference.

In the burgeoning literature seeking to explain our global crisis, when commentators attempt to unearth the basis of the divide between the West and the rest – or, as it seems to be increasingly expressed, Islam and 'our' values – sexuality emerges again and again as a central theme. In a kind of echo of anti-western critiques, champions of the West also seem to believe that sexuality is central to western culture and values. Somehow, and I acknowledge that this is alongside the more explicit objectives of security and access to resources, the global battles of our time are refracted through the prism of sexuality.

I don't want to distance myself from the claims of sexual freedom or even of the image of sex as freedom. My point is not that we should berate ourselves for participating in such a superficial and dehumanising sexual culture. Of course, it may be possible for commodified sexual experience to be enriching and even freeing. However, the investment of so-called western cultures (which may be better described as so-called market democracies) in an opposition between 'our' sexual freedom and 'their' sexual repression shapes our mutual misunderstanding and ongoing conflict(s). The dreams of western sexual freedom shape the manner of western torture. How we can imagine humiliation and pain becomes linked to this imagining of freedom. Most of all, the belief that sexual freedom is ours and that 'they' envy, resent, misunderstand and wish to destroy precisely this most precious and everyday aspect of our culture shapes popular conceptions of the enemy. In the manner of other earlier racialised myths, beliefs about sexuality add to the imaginary embodiment of the demon other.

In *Occidentalism: The West in the Eyes of its Enemies*, Ian Buruma and Avishai Margalit make the claim that sexuality and the position of women hold a pivotal role in tensions between 'western values' and their critics. This is not the most developed aspect of the argument, but rather operates as a repeated aside throughout the larger narrative. 'Look', we are reminded, 'it is all about sex. They envy our freedoms. They want to repress and oppress women.'

> The West is the main target of the enemies of idolatry, even though Islamist political activism is often directed at the oppressive regimes in nominally Muslim countries. One reason for this is the idea of arrogance, manifested in Western imperialism, that is seen as an infringement of the rule of God. The other is about the breaking of sexual taboos – that is about the West as the main corruptor of sexual morality. So the immediate targets of radical Islamism may be regimes in the Middle East and Southeast Asia, but pride and promiscuity, those corrupting forces in the service of human degradation, are the twin reasons that the West is still seen as the prime source of idolatry. (Buruma and Margalit, 2004, 126–7)

The focus for Buruma and Margalit is not only the activity of so-called Islamists, although they do present this group as epitomising the demonisation of the West that they seek to challenge. The project of *Occidentalism* is also to uncover the extent to which this practice has become normalised among Muslim communities, and here sexuality serves to explain the attraction of elements of political Islam for migrant communities in particular.

> Even if they have little idea what the ideal Islamic state should look like, they care deeply about sexual mores, corruption, and traditional family life. Islam, to the believers, is the only source and guardian of traditional collective morality. And sexual morality is largely about women, about regulating female behaviour. This is so because a man's honour is dependent on the behaviour of the women related to him. The issue of women is not marginal; it lies at the heart of Islamic Occidentalism. (Buruma and Margalit, 2004, 128)

Of course, we have little sense of how this intimate knowledge of 'they', those others, is gathered. What is clear is the characterisation that 'they' are given here. This is a description that is careful to avoid accusations of wilful violence, irrational hatred, indifference to the value of human life. Instead, this is a different and quieter version of spotting the Islamist. Here, 'they' are those who value a traditionalism that they do not wholly understand, observant but not theologically knowledgeable, yearning for the stability of a traditional collective morality which may never have existed at all. Buruma's argument is that such people are susceptible to the claims of those who blame the West for the degradations of modern life, degradations embodied as unbridled commerce, sexual licence and a desire to place man above God. Competing beliefs about sexual behaviour become pivotal in this depiction of the fracture lines between communities, nations and cultures.

This is an underlying theme through much of the literature on our global crisis. The West is, in fact, obsessed with sex – but the obsession is with an image of sex as freedom. This celebration of sexual freedom and the apparent rights of women brings together some unlikely players – including those who in the past have opposed feminist demands and berated western societies for the loosening of sexual morality. However, in the context of an imagined global cultural conflict, sexuality is deployed as a symbol of all things western that must be defended. Of course, this development makes sense only in relation to the widespread perception that 'they', those barbaric others, hate 'our' freedoms, our freedom to love and touch and leave and experiment and the freedom of 'our' women to move and love freely. This account of sexual freedom, of a sort, comes to play the role of iconic image of personal freedom. This, combined with 'democracy', is presented as a distillation of western values – what must be defended at all costs.

At the outset, we should be clear that this book is not an attempt at authentic or accurate representation. The point is not that these accounts are a distortion of Islam, the West or anything else. I accept that no one can represent all and that the troubled terrain of cultural competency and battle must be challenged. However, my interest and my job have been the analysis of cultural representations, because I have believed that attentive reading of such ephemeral forms adds to our understanding of how meaning and value are created and ascribed in our world. Now it seems that this task becomes at once more urgent and more dangerous than ever – and more open to misuse and misinterpretation than before. So, to be clear to all readers, my intention here is not to offer a 'true' or better representation of Islam or to uncover the theological continuities or divisions between traditions. My chosen task is to examine key representations of culture and sexuality as they emerge in the West, from many voices, and to suggest that these emanations can help us to understand the reconfiguration of global relations in our time.

Of course, Buruma and Margalit are responding, belatedly and with ill temper, to the long shadow of *Orientalism* (Said, 1979) – and adopting the role of victims of misrepresentation by ill-informed easterners. This reclamation of cultural victimhood echoes trends both within western multiculturalism and in international relations. As many others have remarked, international terrorism is widely portrayed as a direct outcome of the failures of multiculturalism. Gillian Youngs has argued that the War on Terror is also characterised by a confusion and blurring between local, national and international levels of political activity. The sense that incompatible views on sexuality and the position of women embody the fault line between us and them in neighbourhoods, national policies and international relations filters through the representation of the War on Terror. To understand this process we need to think about representations of sexuality and of 'race', and to read these concepts alongside the accounts of international relations and the conduct of war.

The chapters that follow address four aspects of this debate. Chapter 1 reviews the impact of feminism in debates about foreign policy and considers the significance of such widespread misappropriation of feminist language and claims. Chapter 2 moves on to consider the processes of embodiment that emerge in representations of the War on Terror, including a discussion of proper and improper gendering as imagined in this frame. Chapter 3 revisits discussions about state racism and the construction of Muslim men as a racialised threat through techniques of everyday militarisation. Chapter 4 analyses representations of torture carried out in the name of the War on Terror and considers the role of sexuality in practices of torture and in representational traditions. The conclusion brings these ideas together to argue that the circulation of images and rumours of sexualised and racialised violence create a global public of unwilling spectators.

1

The Misuse of Feminism in Foreign Policy

The twenty-first century has seen international and national politics refracted through allegations about culture, belief and antecedence. From 9/11 to the attacks on Afghanistan and Iraq to the overall and unfinished debate about the nature, reach and substance of the War on Terror, the suggestion that the world is divided into antagonistic groups who inhabit incompatible cultures or hold diametrically opposed beliefs has entered the serious businesses of war, diplomacy and public rhetoric. Not for the first time, women, bodies and sexuality have taken on a heightened symbolic role and complex narratives have been constructed that link the three themes and in turn link this assemblage to the responsibilities and choices of states. In common with others (Eisenstein, 2007; Shepherd, 2006), my sense is that this utilisation of concepts of women's place, proper bodies and free and unfree sexuality is not unique but that there are distinctive features in their take-up in our time. The exploitation of an appeal to feminism, however insubstantial and uninformed such an appeal might be, is one aspect of this distinctiveness.

This chapter reconsiders the use of a rhetoric of feminism in the pursuit of the War on Terror. I am using the term 'rhetoric' here to indicate the tactical deployment of the language and style of feminism in order to achieve other strategic goals – in other words, in order to shape the response of the other and the outcomes from an interaction through strategies of persuasive language.

The instigators of the War on Terror, famously, have pointed to the rights of women as a justification for military intervention. The early and much-cited invocations of supposedly feminist solidarity from Laura Bush in her radio address to the nation on 17 November 2001 typify one moment in this process:

> The brutal oppression of women is a central goal of terrorists. … Civilised people throughout the world are speaking out in horror – not only because our hearts break for the women and children in Afghanistan but also because in Afghanistan we see the world the terrorists would like to impose on the rest of us. (Laura Bush, 2001)

George Bush's 2008 BBC interviews, billed explicitly as a review of the 'legacy' of this presidency, also saw Bush respond to the accusation from the Chinese authorities that the US was stuck in Cold War thinking with the assertion that the US was engaged in an ideological struggle with people who were both evil and in thrall to an ideology that targeted the hopeless by refusing rights to women, denying religious freedom and instigating terrorist violence (Bush, 2008). Despite the considerable debate and careful critique mounted by feminists and others, the slogan of women's rights continues to play a talismanic role in Bush's depiction and justification of the War on Terror.

In the War on Terror, the abuse of women and the denial of their public rights has been used as a marker of barbarism and as an indication of societal sickness, a sickness requiring intervention. This could be regarded as another example where insights from development organisations are redeployed as an element of military strategy (Duffield, 2001). While few would deny that the Taliban represented a highly dangerous development for women (and religious minorities and trade unionists and leftists, among others), embedding one version of women's rights in the project of military occupation and western expansion confirms the implication that the West is subduing a type of masculine dysfunction – which, unsurprisingly, invites resistance to western feminism from those wishing to resist such imperial aspirations. Jasmin Zine has described this in terms of the challenges facing Muslim feminists from the simultaneous threats of 'gendered Islamophobia' (Zine, 2004) and 'religious extremism and puritan discourses that authorize equally limiting narratives of Islamic womanhood' (Zine, 2006, 27). One aspect of the War on Terror has been this battle over the meaning and ownership of the idea of women's rights. This chapter examines some feminist responses to the War on Terror and considers what is at stake when well-known opponents of women's rights utilise feminist rhetoric for other ends.

Rhetorics of feminism and the War on Terror

The attacks of 11 September 2001 were met with many varieties of horror, surprise and outrage. However, among these understandable reactions, there was a less familiar appeal to popular feminist sensibilities in some highly publicised and early responses (for a discussion of this see Shepherd, 2006; Steans, 2008; Croft, 2006). Such statements were all the more surprising given that key speakers, most obviously those affiliated to the Bush administration, had been openly and strongly opposed to any extension of the rights of women at home or abroad. There was certainly little indication that the public embracing of liberal feminist demands and ideals could serve any populist or electoral purpose. If anything, the Bush administration in particular had been elected through the mobilisation of a coalition of forces that included elements who remained highly antagonistic to feminist demands in any form. The Bush administration has been heavily reliant on the support of evangelical Christian groups and other representatives of the Christian right. One price of this alliance has been the insertion of actively anti-feminist initiatives into the business of mainstream government (Kaplan, 2005). In this context, the public rhetoric of the War on Terror as a battle for women's rights has been regarded with suspicion, if not outright ridicule, by feminist activists and scholars.

> The irony of George W. Bush presenting himself as a champion of women's rights was not lost on feminist commentators and activists in the United States and elsewhere who pointed out that neo-conservatives – often in alliance with conservative and fundamentalist Islamic states – had actively sought to roll back key planks of the international women's rights agenda over the past decade in the interest of rescuing the traditional – read patriarchal – American family. (Steans, 2008, 164)

Certainly, feminists in the US and elsewhere were under no illusions about the attitude of the Bush administration to policy issues impacting on women. Internationally, the United States continues to refuse to sign the Convention on the Elimination of All Forms of Discrimination Against Women (CEDAW), effectively blocking its implementation, and under Bush there has been a withdrawal of US aid to sexual health and family planning programmes that provide information about abortion (Kaplan, 2005). Within the US, the Bush administration has closed the Women's Bureau in the Labor

Department – thus dismantling the apparatus to track gender and pay (Eisenstein, 2006, 195) and closed the White House Women's Office. Audiences with some knowledge of these matters have regarded the use of feminist claims in the War on Terror as no more than a cynical cover for a business-as-usual imperialist foray to safeguard both access to resources and geopolitical leverage.

However, despite this, the intensive media circulation of the claim that this war was to protect women has shaped public debate on these issues. Media audiences in the US and beyond are unlikely to be well-informed about the detail of US government policy. Issues such as the blocking of obscure international treaties or changes in the detail of aid distribution do not translate easily to headlines, in either domestic or international media.

> The story about women's human rights has been reproduced by US media which have largely, until recently, rallied to the cause as spun by the White House. The evocation of liberated Western women and oppressed Muslim women has been useful in the project of casting the United States as a beacon of civilisation and in constructing, reinforcing and reproducing an 'us versus them' polarity between the West and the Islamic world. (Steans, 2008, 160)

There has been considerable criticism of this rhetoric and framework, with a growing feminist literature challenging the expedient use of feminist rhetoric and the pretended defence of women. However, in popular discourse, the claims of Muslim repression and western liberation of women continue to circulate. In particular, the stance of the US group, the Feminist Majority Foundation, in supporting the attacks on Afghanistan as necessary for the liberation of Afghani women, served to confirm to an unschooled international audience that this was a war informed by (US) feminism.

There has been no shortage of feminist challenges to this disreputable misuse of feminist claims by non-feminist forces. Gillian Youngs summarises some of these critiques when she writes, 'when western women hear their governments engage in such warrior speak about eastern women, embedded within it are gendered assumptions about western women's inferior social status' (Youngs, 2006, 11).

However seductive the narrative of rescue can be, especially when structured around representations of veiled, voiceless and utterly othered women in poor parts of the world, feminists in the West have learned that cultural projects that assume that foreign women need to be saved have consequences for women at home. The story of rescued women anywhere relies on the idea that women everywhere are less than men, helpless victims waiting to be saved. In connection to this, Stabile and Kumar have argued that the Bush administration represented women's equality in the West as a natural part of 'western humanist values', in the process erasing the struggles of generations of feminists to achieve such rights (Stabile and Kumar, 2005).

This has been the defence of feminists in many places. The War on Terror may reference feminism and ventriloquise feminist concerns and goals, but this is an instrumental appropriation by those who have no interest in or commitment to feminism. Feminism is a veil, or in Zillah Eisenstein's phrase, a decoy to avert attention from the actual activity and focus of this war (Eisenstein, 2007).

However, despite this concern to delegitimise the feminist claims of the War on Terror, the place of feminism and the implications for the status of women are far from decided. Defenders of the invasions of Afghanistan and Iraq continue to suggest that regime change by force has been in the interests of women (Bush, 2008). Commentators continue to evaluate the position of women as an indicator of successful nation-building or post-war reconstruction (Oates, 2006). Whatever the actuality of feminist participation or influence, the War on Terror remains an endeavour that is shaped in dialogue with at least an idea of feminism. My argument here is not that feminism or feminists have been complicit with the activities of the War on Terror – for most, the opposite is the case and feminist activists have taken high-profile and vocal roles in anti-war and civil liberties campaigns in many parts of the world. However, despite this, the use of stolen feminist rhetoric has continued to form an important aspect of the claims of the War on Terror and this claim has continued to gain some acceptance in popular media. For example, in early 2008, at a time of intensive domestic debate about the continuing presence of British troops in Afghanistan, the UK media was filled with concerns about the case of a young man sentenced to death allegedly for downloading and distributing a report about women's rights (Sengupta, 2008). The central message of this coverage was horror that such things continue to happen when we went there to defend women's rights. Although such media coverage brings a necessary corrective to the US-led coalition claim that Afghani women have been liberated by military intervention, it reveals a continuing belief that the original military offensive was intended to 'save' the women of Afghanistan and a disappointment that this rescue project has not been achieved. Although many parties doubt the intentions and ability of Bush, there appears to be a widespread acceptance that military intervention in pursuit of women's rights is necessary and desirable, if carried out effectively.

The War on Terror as yet another ethnic war

In addition to this discussion of the desirability and effectivity of war for women's rights, the amalgamated activities of the War on Terror are characterised by a range of gender work familiar from analyses of earlier nationalist wars. Feminist scholars have insisted in the debates of recent decades that the business of states, nationalisms and war are all highly gendered and shaped by and shaping of gender identities. In a famous collection, Nira Yuval-Davis and Floya Anthias introduced this idea with the words:

> We claim that central dimensions of the roles of women are constituted around the relationships of collectivities to the state. We also claim that central dimensions of the relationships between collectivities and the state are constituted around the roles of women. (Yuval-Davis and Anthias, 1989, 2)

Importantly for further debate in the area, the authors go on to identify five areas in which women have tended to participate in ethnic and national processes. These are listed as:

(a) biological reproducers of ethnic collectivities;
(b) reproducers of the boundaries of ethnic/national groups;
(c) participating centrally in the ideological reproduction of the collec-tivity and as transmitters of its culture;
(d) signifiers of ethnic/national differences – as a focus and symbol in ideological discourses used in the construction, reproduction and transformation of ethnic/national categories;
(e) participants in national, economic, political and military struggles. (Yuval-Davis and Anthias, 1989, 7)

The War on Terror assumes a slightly different form from the conflict situations imagined in this typology. However, the checklist serves as an important reminder of the multiple and well-known roles assigned to women in the varied processes of nation building. Despite the disavowal of both ethnic exclusivity and national interest, the deployment of ideas of femininity and its place in a cultural community pervade the rhetoric of the War on Terror. Although in this narrative there is an active refusal to allot the role of breeder to women in the West, because this reduction to reproductive function is portrayed as part of the barbarism of the enemy, the other four points identified by Yuval-Davis and Anthias can be transferred to the project of the War on Terror with little adaptation. However much it is denied that this war operates around boundaries of ethnicity, the repeated claim that it is a feminist war requires women in/of the West to embody a significant boundary between us and them. The presentation of a particular culture of westernisation and consumerism as central to feminism collapses the conduct and aspirations of women in/of the West into the supposed ideological reproduction of the collectivity and into a signifier of ethnic/cultural difference. Women's ongoing struggles for everyday freedoms are appropriated into the racialised war project and presented as, if not quite an ethnic culture, at least an explicit demonstration of our values, the very values that are under attack and that must be defended. In these circumstances, it is unsurprising that women also play a variety of roles in the conflict situations that arise from the War on Terror, with plenty of examples of women performing military, administrative and propaganda roles for coalition forces as well as of women organising in the peace movement, with other women transnationally playing roles in the various resistance, insurgent, nationalist and religious movements that oppose US and allied forces.

There may be no agreement about the ethnic character of the War on Terror, but the deployment of ideas about the role of women echoes more familiar projects of ethnic boundary-marking. Others have remarked on the manner in which women have come to be used as a symbolic marker in the struggle between 'us' and 'them' (Al-Ali, 2005), and on the depiction of western culture as being typified by multicultural tolerance, consumer citizenship and sexual freedoms that allow pleasurable heterosexuality and inclusion in the national narrative for lesbian, gay, bisexual and transgender people (Puar, 2006). In these claims, there is the implication of a shared culture among 'us', and although this shared space admits diverse identities, it also disciplines members of the group into conformity and reproduction of group myths. The vision of western culture as being identified by unique characteristics of tolerance for ethnic and sexual diversity and freedom for women becomes a version of a nationalist project, and women are deployed to project and further this vision, occupying roles not dissimilar to those described by the account of processes of nationalist and ethnic projects. The fact that this assertion of superior group identity presents itself as above the backward claims of ethnicity does not prevent an active racialisation of the enemy.

Feminist thinking and transnational understanding

From the vantage point of feminist scholarship, this continuing investment in supremacist models of understanding can seem bemusing. Such delusions of emancipation and cultural superiority have been critiqued by feminist scholars across a range of disciplines (Spivak, 1987; Eisenstein, 2004; Mohanty, 1988; Alexander, 1996). Feminism has been unmade and remade in the light of these troubling but important disagreements, and feminist approaches to understanding the world have become imbued with the legacy of such debates.

In Britain the small gains of so-called ethical foreign policy have been formed in dialogue of a sort with feminism. Although after Iraq it is hard to think of Blair's Britain as anything other than a protagonist in the new imperialism, the ethical aspirations of such bloody endeavours cannot be understood without some attention to the political energies and alliances that informed the centre-left project of New Labour. These included a resurrection of a reading of Christian Socialism that portrayed intervention against evil as an unquestionable moral duty (Leach, 2002; Huntington and Bale, 2002); the development of a 'third way' conception of global relations that portrayed the terrain of patriotism and the banal popular nationalism of the everyday as part of what must be wrested from the right if the overall project of creating a new hegemonic bloc beyond left and right was to succeed (Giddens, 1998); and the influence of feminist sensibilities among a number of central players.

Although there has been considerable debate about the actual impact of New Labour for women (Coote, 2000), many would argue that the somewhat uneasy political alliances that led to a (New)

Labour election victory in 1997 included influence from feminists and feminism (Russell, 2005). Key figures in the Blair court had come through the equality and other battles of local government during the Thatcher years – and this group included a number of high-profile cabinet ministers (Rawnsley, 2000). The unexpected reinvigoration of Christian Socialist elements in the party – an affiliation that has become more contested as others in this largely left-leaning grouping have opposed both the war in Iraq and wider failures to address social inequality – may appear to echo the political alliances forged by the Bush administration, but in fact the role of Christian rhetoric in the political life of Britain has been quite distinct from the content and methods of the US Christian Right. There is some evidence of US-influenced evangelical groups spreading into the UK, including through the so-called sponsorship of state schools (Harris, 2005) and entry into public office (Ekklesia, 2008). However, UK Christian groups do not represent the level of organisation and influence associated with US politics. Tony Blair's references to his own Christian beliefs have been a cause of concern and ridicule (BBC News, 2007) and, despite the creeping influence of highly conservative forms of Christian belief among New Labour cabinet ministers, there is little evidence of an organised *Christian* vote in British politics (as opposed to voting defined by local communal or sectarian divisions). As a result, Britain has not paralleled Bush's attacks on women's organisations and campaigns. Instead, there has been an attempt to fold the concerns of women into more instrumental policy objectives such as addressing low earnings and enabling welfare claimants and lone parents to re-enter the job market (Coote, 2000), and an accommodation of feminist activists within some structures of the government and party (Russell, 2005). Some, such as McRobbie, have launched a trenchant critique of the manner in which (post)feminist rhetoric has been mobilised to discipline young women into effective and unresisting market participation (McRobbie, 2007). However, overall, the claim that this was a humanitarian war for the rights of women and others has served in Britain as an explanation for an otherwise seemingly inexplicable alliance with this most right-wing of US presidencies. Whatever the opposition to the war itself, this implementation by force of women's rights continues to be regarded as a laudable goal.

Feminism via the academy

The widespread impact of feminist debate and politics from the 1970s onwards, not least through the influence of university teachers and other researchers on generations of women and men who now populate significant governmental institutions, has created a cadre of professionals whose training has taken place in dialogue with feminist thinking and modes of understanding. In significant areas such as poverty reduction, agricultural reform, health, security studies and global stability and governance, feminist scholars and activists have shifted the focus of research and policy to such an extent that feminist goals can be cited as indicators of policy success (see gender and development organisation BRIDGE at http://www.bridge.ids.ac.uk/) .

These are developments that cannot be dismissed as fake feminism, in the manner of recent proclamations about the welfare of the women of Afghanistan and Iraq. Instead, this is work that shows the influence of feminist involvement, however carefully negotiated. If we consider some well-known examples of gender equality goals being pursued through foreign policy, it is not long before familiar and longstanding feminist demands appear among the technical requirements of development or co-operation.

One US initiative, the Millennium Challenge Corporation, has taken the unprecedented step of making compliance with gender equality concerns a qualification for funding. Thus Lesotho has been encouraged to change the domestic law that reduces a married woman to the status of a child before resubmitting its application for development funding from MCC (Women's Edge, 2007). Such initiatives are explained as a response to the revelation that gender inequality is a barrier to market participation and economic liberalisation – yet the requirement to grant legal rights clearly does benefit the women of Lesotho, regardless of this desire to transform them into ideal market actors.

As development becomes increasingly rationalised as a component of security, the potential transnational turbulence from local gender inequalities has come to be viewed with concern. An excess of young men in any population, including the bulge caused by active selection of male children in some areas, has come to be regarded as a security threat in the making (Hudson and Den Boer, 2004; for a critique see Hendrixson, 2004).

As a result, a version of feminist analysis now comes to inform security debates, not necessarily because the moral weight of feminist claims has been recognised but because the turbulence that can occur as a result of the interaction of gender inequality and deep social division and social inequality has come to be regarded as a transnational threat. Bizarrely, transnational feminist scholarship comes to be of interest to the world's powers.

The manner in which feminist knowledge has developed can make this work appear useful to those who wish to capture the simultaneous linkedness and diversity of global living.

> Feminisms have a unity which is also simultaneously diverse. It is multiple and continues to multiply. As such, feminisms is the most inclusive theory of social justice that I know. (Eisenstein, 2004, 219)

The problem for women in/of the 'West' is that the name of our feminism is being taken in vain by those who historically have had little interest in our advancement. However, the claims that are being made in our name are not, in fact, easily distinguishable from those articulated by 'real' feminists. In this sense, as stated above, this imperial deployment is not pretend feminism, because the influence of feminist scholarship, lobbying and activism is readily apparent in its articulation. For example, the UK's Foreign and Commonwealth Office document 'Inclusive Government: Mainstreaming Gender Equality into Foreign Policy' outlines a range of measures that can be used to promote gender equality in the conduct of Foreign Office business. The suggestions include: initiatives to enable women's political participation; the use of gender impact assessments; promoting education for girls and women; attention to the gender implications of local problems, including expectations around cultures of masculinity; developing positive representations of women. Each suggested initiative bears the marks of feminist thinking and activism – this is something like a policy attempt to address Cynthia Enloe's distillation of feminist enquiry, 'Where are the women?'

Although I am deeply suspicious about the deployment of feminist goals in the conduct of international politics, I cannot say with any honesty that the aspirations of 'Inclusive Government' are objectionable or even obviously tied to western interests. I may be uncomfortable with the MCC fixation on women's market participation, but

I cannot disagree with their wish to change discriminatory laws. The problem, then, is the context in which such claims are presented and pursued. These are not the wrong things to ask for necessarily, it is only that to ask for such things in the shadow of military occupation compromises the pursuit of women's rights.

Transnational feminism and rethinking alliances again

The misuse of an idea of women's rights by the US and its allies has reignited debates among feminist activists and scholars about transnational relations, local struggles, and the possibility of feminist movements that can collaborate respectfully across borders. Some of this discussion has taken the form of a refusal of the terms both of imperial feminism and of patriarchal nativism.

> Both the colonialist and ... the counter-colonialist representation of Arab women need to be challenged. Arab women's need for positive change in their lives is neither more nor less than the need of women for positive change anywhere else in the world. (Al-Hassan Golley, 2004, 522)

This sentiment is echoed many times in the course of the War on Terror, from activist groups (Brodsky, 2003) to feminist scholars (Muaddi Darraj, 2002) to policy advisers. In the process, there has been a creeping suggestion that feminism may not, in fact, be antithetical to nationalism or other more local ethnic demands. Perhaps predictably, the rapid re-emergence of an openly imperial vision of the world and of the accompanying rights of powerful nations has triggered a re-assessment of the relationship between feminist and nationalist aspirations in less powerful parts of the world:

> nationalism must be conceived as involving dual goals: first, externally, it is to attain veritable self-determination of the nation, and the recognition and respect for the nation as an equal partner among nations in the international arena; and second, internally, it is to secure an inner environ-ment in which the members of the nation can enjoy equality amongst themselves and work with one another to promote collective prosperity. ... These two goals are not separate, but intimately connected. (Sedou Herr, 2003, 149)

While anti-imperialist and anti-war feminists in affluent nations, understandably, have focused their energies on refusing the nationalist call for women's obedience and allegiance (Eisenstein, 2004; Cockburn,

2007), in other parts of the world other pressures are shaping feminist responses. After a period when feminist defences of nationalism were somewhat muted, if existing at all, the apparently renewed threat of external intervention has reintroduced debates about national sovereignty to the field. The plea to respect each nation's right to struggle for self-determination and to conduct the struggle for full and equal national citizenship as a dialogue between its members makes sense in a world where powerful nations have reasserted their entitlement to intervene against others who are perceived to threaten them or to violate their codes of human rights. In such a context, the claim that feminist and nationalist campaigns can be complementary and should be respected as such has a heightened significance.

The argument that feminist struggles must be shaped and led by the concerns and cultural understandings of those who belong to the space or community in question has been asserted by black, Third World and other feminists many times before (Alexander, 1996; Moraga and Anzaldua, 1983). Alongside this, it has been argued that feminists must be attentive to the distinction between zones of peace and zones of conflict (Jacoby, 2005, 4). This is because while the relative peace and prosperity of some locations shapes a certain set of feminist interventions, for other women politicisation takes place in 'the broader contexts of civil-ethnic conflicts and developing states' (Jacoby, 2005, 4).

> In conflict zones, women mobilize alongside their men, whether to liberate their society from colonial or post-colonial oppression, to campaign for national self-determination, or to partake in the process of democratization.

This, according to Jacoby's analysis, often involves participation in violent conflict and a deferment of struggles for individual rights in favour of support for the collective struggle. Although such a formulation can appear to replay earlier tensions between socialism and feminism or nationalism and feminism, where the claims of women were regarded as subservient to the larger struggle, there is political and analytic merit in understanding the particular contours that shape the politicisation and priorities of women activists in different locations.

The resurrection of this claim could be read as indicative of some overlapping concerns. There is the assertion that we, too, are real feminists and able to determine our own goals and understanding of equality. There is also a recognition that the pursuit of feminist goals has become part of the machinery of statecraft and that to lay claim to this area is to assert the right to be an interlocutor of government, or at least of government in waiting. There is also a defence against external intervention, not because all is well but because only insiders can make effective change. This last doubles as a plea against the appropriation of feminist, human rights or other movements as a justification for unfriendly intervention or aggression against more vulnerable societies:

> Third World feminists are prime examples of 'social critics.' Third World feminists are firmly ensconced in their own culture, not only in the banal sense that their identities are intricately tied to their culture, but also in the sense that their particular feminist agenda makes sense only within their own particular culture. They become aware of the necessity for feminist movement because they witness or experience particular sexist and misogynist practices and their detrimental effects on women; as far as these practices determine the feminist agenda, feminists navigate within the parameters set by their culture. (Sedou Herr, 2003, 151)

In fact, and despite the considerable efforts to come to a mutually respectful appreciation of differences between feminists, it is hard to imagine a feminist politics that could remain so tidily within the terms of local concerns. The argument that attempts to reconcile feminism and some nationalist projects is itself shaped by the realisation that the status of women and the claims of feminism have become inextricably linked into debates about the boundaries of national sovereignty and the role of international institutions and/or NGOs. The argument that Third World or other feminists have the expertise to mobilise effectively in their own locations only makes sense as a rebuttal against meddling carried out in the name of international feminism. It is precisely the unstoppable global reach of feminist claims and interpretations of competing varieties that pushes some women to defend the particularity of their own political struggles. The point is not that there is no transnational language of feminism, only discrete local struggles, but that such a transnational language is not free from the other power imbalances and embarrassments of transnational relations, including the shameless and yet seemingly effective appropriation of feminist rhetoric for other ends. Nadje Al-Ali suggests that the most effective way to make space for the shared project of feminism is to acknowledge the disproportionate power of western women in transnational settings and therefore to mute agendas and approaches that appear too identified with the West. Al-Ali puts this more politely:

> One way to sensitively support women is to change the language from a feminist rights approach to one emphasising education, training and participation in reconstruction, thereby appealing to a modernist–developmental discourse. The other major strategy is to link women with organisations, experts and initiatives in other countries in the region or in the Muslim world. Based on research I carried out among women's organisations in Egypt, for example, I found that women felt much more empowered by the exchange of experiences and training with non-Western women activists. (Al-Ali, 2005, 757)

After feminism has been ripped apart, reworked and rebuilt to accommodate and respect not only the diversity of women but the variation in gendering cultures and the different yet equal contextual pressures faced by activists in different places, few have much appetite for a reopening of self-destructive modes of debate. Instead it seems that hard times are forcing the terms of debate, so that earlier rancour and name-calling have been replaced, for some, by a recognition that shared interests and languages exist that link feminists from different locations. However, instead of a return to some triumphal universalism, this is a shared agenda that cannot be pursued without attention to local contexts, including the important context of anti-western sentiment.

Built into these developments in feminist debate is the admission that the category of 'woman' is constructed and adapted through transnational processes, not only along the endless axis of male–female, but also as an important entity in the drama of globalised relations. Chandra Mohanty explains this point:

> Just as there is an Anglo-American masculinity produced in and by discourses of globalization, it is important to ask what the corresponding femininities being produced are. Clearly there is the ubiquitous global teenage girl factory worker, the domestic worker, and the sex worker. There is also the migrant/immigrant service worker, the refugee, the victim of war crimes, the woman-of-color prisoner who happens to be a mother and drug user, the consumer-housewife, and so on. There is also the mother-of-the-nation/religious bearer of traditional culture and morality. (Mohanty, 2003, 527)

Mohanty's earlier and highly influential essay 'Under Western Eyes' argued the need both to develop autonomous accounts of women's struggles across the world that are historically and politically grounded and to mount an internal critique of the imperial mindset of western feminism (Mohanty, 1988). Her recent revisiting of this work and reconsideration of its arguments serves as an interesting document of larger shifts in feminist debate. Now Mohanty claims the vigour and ambition of the anti-globalisation movement for feminism, admitting that these campaigns are not explicitly feminist in aim but instead are informed by feminist politics and peopled by women who are shaped by feminism of an anti-colonial kind.

> While feminists have been involved in the antiglobalization movement from the start, however, this has not been a major organizing locus for women's movements nationally in the West/North. It has, however, always been a locus of struggle for women of the Third World/South because of their location. Again, this contextual specificity should constitute the larger vision. Women of the Two-Thirds World have always organized against the devastations of globalized capital, just as they have always historically organized anticolonial and antiracist movements. In this sense they have always spoken for humanity as a whole. (Mohanty, 2003, 516)

The debate within feminism appears to have shifted from arguments about who is speaking for whom inappropriately, about who is projecting an orientalist and objectifying vision onto others, about who is homogenising the category of woman in order to privilege their own experience and position. Now the claim is that feminism of the correct anti-capitalist anti-imperialist nuance can articulate a more general longing for justice. Feminism has learned through bitter experience and considerable in-fighting that the commonality of an apparently shared identity is not enough to build sustainable political alliances or to agree a shared programme or vision. Now feminist scholars argue that feminism can teach us to produce more effective analyses of how and where injustice happens and perhaps even suggest a model of co-operative working against such horrors.

Feminism, multiculturalism and the limits of sovereignty

In a highly contentious and much-discussed book, Susan Moller Okin famously asks 'Is multiculturalism bad for women?' This question and the range of responses and refutations that it elicits demonstrate a key shift in understandings of feminism and the relation of feminism to other social movements. The framing of the question indicates the fraught space of this debate and its implications: that liberal tolerance of some cultural communities is a tolerance of the oppression and suppression of women; that the cultural and social ambitions of some groups are antithetical to the interests of women; that the appeal to women in the West to adapt to newcomers and their ways is a demand that they give up on their own hard-won social freedoms. In fact the analysis of such issues has become a busy subset of academic and political life (Okin, 1999; Reitman, 2005; Nussbaum, 2000; Young, 1990).

My interest here is not in the competing claims of those for and against the proposition – these are rehearsed thoroughly in Okin's collection – but in the implications of such a debate. Okin responds to her opponents with this paragraph, clarifying her proposition and alluding to its implications:

> I argue that many cultures oppress some of their members, in particular women, and that they are often able to socialize these oppressed members so that they accept, without question, their designated cultural status. I argue, therefore, that in the context of liberal states, when cultural or religious groups claim special rights – whether to be exercised by them together as a group or individually as members of that group – attention should be paid to the status of women within the culture or religion. This means that it is not enough for those representing the liberal state simply to listen to the requests of the self-styled group leaders. They must enquire into the point of view of the women, and take especially seriously the perspective of the younger women. (Moller Okin, 1999, 117)

There is no space here to examine the contention that cultural or religious groups enjoy special rights in liberal societies. This claim has been repeated extensively in recent debates about the alleged non-viability of multiculturalism. More significant for our purposes is the manner in which these repressive cultures are portrayed. These are groups in thrall to that modern-day folk-devil, the self-styled community leader. That heady combination of charismatic rhetoric and collective policing creates a group identity that inculcates obedience in its members and that, in the face of hostile majority reactions, is defended even by the most downtrodden members of the group (for critiques of the role of community leaders, see Kundnani,

2002; Hundal, 2007). I don't deny that membership in a variety of cultural groupings may lead individuals to act against their own interests – or that women may be particularly vulnerable to such destructive bargains, not least because their ability to act autonomously and without regard for the social consequences can be limited by caring responsibilities. However, the overall argument that some people cannot exercise the self-definition that open societies offer to other members is a difficult one. There are many areas of life where individuals appear to act against their own interests, whether that be in relation to the maintenance of health, the recreational use of alcohol or other drugs, sexual safety or romantic dangers, allegiance to employers and governments that further their exploitation, the whole gamut of risky behaviour that characterises social life. Any intervention against the freely taken choices of some minority of citizens is likely to be shaped by the power disparities between those who intervene and those who are judged. However contentious the notion of free choice might be here, any attempt to suggest that the choices of some are less free than those of others will be overwritten by other troubling social relations such as class and race. Once again, the world-view of the most privileged is the one most likely to be imposed.

Feminist scholars have worked hard to challenge the false polarisation of this debate, with key commentators arguing that cultures are not monolithic and unassailable, that it is possible to formulate demands for women's rights without colluding in the demonisation of groups suffering racism, and that the framing of the debate in these terms is a disservice to both feminism and multiculturalism (for an example, see the reports from 'Beyond "Feminism Versus Multiculturalism"', 2006). However, in relation to global participation in the War on Terror, this alleged incompatibility between the rights of women and the claims of cultural minorities continues to play an important role.

My book argues that the War on Terror must be analysed as both a series of military interventions and an ongoing campaign to transform the terms of civilian life within nations. Few national governments have supported the US/UK invasion of Iraq. However, far more have pledged their support in the War on Terror – and demonstrated this through their internal practices of government, often in a manner that extended state powers to repress local dissent (Whitaker, 2007). The associative chain linking terrorism, extremism, the repression of women, and minority cultures has proved more influential in this process than any number of dubious reports about weapons of mass destruction. In relation to this, Liz Fekete analyses the impact across Europe of this reinvigorated state racism operating under the pretence of defending women:

> the realigned Right – whose elements range from post-fascists to liberals and even some social democrats – is using state power to reinforce fears about 'aliens' and put into place legal and administrative structures that discriminate against Muslims. ... Central to such a process is a generalised suspicion of Muslims, who are characterised as holding on to an alien culture that, in its opposition to homosexuality and gender equality, threatens core European values. (Fekete, 2006, 2)

The battle to defend 'our' way of life is not only fought in Afghanistan and Iraq – this is a cultural battle in which states are mobilising a range of repressive measures, including increasingly violent and punitive methods of immigration control, in order to control, contain and expel the potentially terrorist other, an otherness seen to be embodied by all Muslims and those who can be (mis)taken to be Muslim. These initiatives reference the alleged threat to the rights of women, lesbian, gay, bisexual and trans communities and to overall social harmony from Muslims who are becoming, it is argued, ever more extreme and demanding. 'The bizarre logic seems to be that the best way to counter possible discrimination against women ... is by bringing in laws that discriminate against ethnic minorities (i.e., Muslims)' (Fekete, 2006, 8). A supposed defence of the values of equality comes to be mobilised as a justification for state repression, most of all in the persecution of migrants. Expectations of the due process of law or of natural justice disappear before the allegedly urgent need to defend 'our' way of life, coded as the rights of women (see Fekete, 2006 for a detailed account of this across Europe). The emotive claim that 'they' wish to brutalise 'our' women and children serves to gather consent for another ratcheting up of discretionary state powers.

There is an all too obvious parallel with challenges to international law in the formulation of (some) feminist challenges to multi-culturalism. Critiques of 'humanitarian imperialism' argue that the recent rush to use military means to pursue human rights goals serves to reproduce existing power inequalities (Bricmont, 2006; Chandler, 2006). David Chandler explains this possibility as stemming from a substantial change in the conception of foreign policy in the last decades of the twentieth century. The widespread mobilisation of a notion of human rights that stood apart, ostensibly, from the realpolitik of interests and alliances led also to the emergence of the ideology of humanitarian interventionism. 'While leading Western states are acquiring special privileges of hegemony, other states are losing the basic rights of sovereignty' (Chandler, 2006, 246).

Chandler's argument is based on the protections of international law and the special place given to sovereign states in this conception and I do not pretend that 'cultures' can or should be granted their own version of sovereignty. It is clear that a significant critique of multiculturalism has been that minority cultures appear to claim sovereignty over their members, at the expense of both the formal claims of state citizenship and the individual interests of members. However, it does seem that attacks on demonised cultural communities have taken on the rhetoric of humanitarian interventionism, despite the poor fit between this metaphor from international relations and interactions in a diverse polity between members of so-called cultural groups.

> Promoting the interests of the ethical 'Other' – the human rights victim – is a sign of the exhaustion of modern politics; an indication that political elites have given up on the project of taking society forward. (Chandler, 2006, 252)

Chandler alleges that the move towards ethical foreign policy and the claiming of human rights as the central motivation behind international actions, including military intervention, is an indication of the retreat from collectivity or any aspiration towards shared goals. In this, Chandler appears to echo the myriad commentators who identify a moral confusion at the heart of western cultures. This, allegedly, is the outcome of godlessness, liberalism, sexual freedoms and/or marketised greed, depending on your chosen monster (for two examples from the British right see Phillips, 2006; Gove, 2006). As a result of the deep confusion and dissatisfaction that lie at the centre of the western project, some new rallying cry must be found to galvanise and redirect the cynicism of pampered yet atomised western subjects. Shifting attention to a needy victimised other whose need places an obligation on us to intervene appears to serve the purpose of binding us together in a shared and, better still, ethical project.

Although Chandler is describing the advent of new approaches towards foreign policy and the resulting erosion of agreements about international law, there is something in his account reminiscent of debates about the inadequacies of multiculturalism. Britain has been plagued in recent years by seemingly endless speculation about the terms and content of British values and the various threats such values may be facing from migrants, Islam and the indifference of the general population (see Gordon Brown's speech of 27 February 2007; for an alternative view see Ware, 2007).

Such discussion reveals nothing so much as a confusion over what if anything might provide a sense of collectivity to lonely citizens. The lament for lost Britishness is both the most recent incarnation of anti-foreigner populist propaganda and the articulation of a larger fear that there is nothing that binds members of this society together, not even that cheapest of rallying cries, nation (Gilroy, 2004). In these circumstances the transferral of interventionist rhetoric from transnational to domestic arenas enables the claim that failing communities, like failing states, demand ethical intervention however unlawful and ruthless such intervention may appear, because not to intervene is to leave these people as needy victims.

In practice, such interventions that undo recognised legal process are not made in order to protect the rights of women and children. Although the treatment of women and children is presented often as the issue that 'proves' the need for unorthodox intervention, the erosions of legal process that characterise anti-terrorism initiatives have not yet been echoed in other areas of law.

The contentious provisions of anti-terrorism practices, on the other hand, have been linked to the alleged failures of multiculturalism and the need to institute parallel provisions for those who cannot or will not adhere to the contract of national belonging. The justification of such extreme measures as detention without trial, the use of evidence extracted through torture, the creation of categories of people who appear to fall outside the everyday protections of due legal process are all presented as ethical interventions, required at once as a pre-emptive strike against these internal enemies and as an emergency measure to protect both minority and majority communities. The central contention that some nations/cultures/communities have placed themselves outside of the protection of law, autonomy and sovereignty due to their own internal weaknesses and failings has taken a similar form in both local and international debates.

It is not suggested here that there is no problem with the treatment of women under some of the targeted regimes. However, equally, it is no surprise to feminists when authoritarian regimes call on men to curtail the freedoms of women, whether this is in the name of religion, national health and security or the well-being of children and families. In the light of the virulence of anti-Islamic proclamations across western societies, it is also worth remembering that others also claim a right to curtail the freedoms of women and to propagate hatred against sexual minorities in the name of their cultures. The Vatican continues to demonise contraception, despite pleas to recognise the impact of such rulings on the behaviour and health outcomes of poor Catholics around the world. Instructions guiding entrance to seminary education not only debar 'those who practise homosexuality, present deeply rooted homosexual tendencies or support the so-called gay culture' (Tatchell, 2005), they also state that homosexual acts are 'grave sins', 'objectively disordered', 'intrinsically immoral' and 'contrary to natural law' (see also Israely, 2005). George Bush and his allies from the Christian Right propagate a vision of sexual relations and (non)access to contraception that serves to tie women to their biological destiny. As a result of the economic and political power of the US, these beliefs impact on the distribution of development aid and funding for scientific research (Kaplan, 2005; International Women's Health Coalition, 2004). Ultra-orthodox Jewish protesters in Israel protest against gay pride marches through Jerusalem and are suspected of having caused a bomb explosion to disrupt the 2007 parade (Lis, 2007). The old themes of family, duty, marriage and monogamy, all enforced through the suppression of women and the persecution of sexual minorities, circulate through the religious revivals or nationalist defences of many locations. Not all are paraded as examples of the barbaric backwardness of that culture; neither are they referenced as justification for pre-emptive military attack or punitive state intervention.

What is this War on Terror feminism?

For decades, feminist theory has been considering the challenges raised by women's diverse locations and experiences. Arguably, it is this question that lies at the heart of feminist theory. This is intellectual work that has been motivated and informed by the urgent questions of what it is to be a woman and of how women might organise to change their circumstances. The competing and some-times incompatible priorities of different women have been the underlying theme through generations of debate, from attempts to quantify the value of domestic labour to calls for socialist feminism, from the porn wars to the critiques of black feminism, lesbian feminism and postcolonial feminism. The allegation that any particular feminist project is imperialising in either approach or ambition cuts deep. Few feminist activists are willing to defend a universalist conception of feminism. Instead the energies of recent times have been devoted to uncovering methods of building a feminism that can encompass difference: 'we know that there is an imperative need to address the concerns of women around the world in the historicized particularity of their relationship to multiple patriarchies as well as to international economic hegemonies' (Grewal and Kaplan, 1994, 17).

It is not my intention to replay these debates about the alleged if unintentional imperialism of feminist theory and activism. This terrain has been extensively, perhaps too extensively, mined already. My interest is in another kind of imperial feminism, one where it is not an unwary feminism that has become contaminated by imperialist ambition but where fairly explicit and unrepentant forms of modern-day imperialism unexpectedly profess feminism to be among the informing philosophies and motivating factors in these endeavours.

The shifts in practice in foreign policy and development that are influenced by feminism, inasmuch as they exist, continue to be characterised by a feminism that gives primacy to the structuring role of gender at the expense of other social relations. This can take place even when there is an acknowledgement of the place of difference and of the diversity of women, because this is a political and episte-mological choice about what is central to the world. Chowdhry and Nair make this point in relatively gentle ways:

> although critical IR [international relations] interrogates many of the assumptions of conventional IR, it nevertheless fails, with some exceptions, to systematically address some of the erasures of the latter [social relations] such as the intersectionality of race, class, and gender in the production of power in IR. ... while feminist IR challenges the

gendered assumptions of both mainstream and critical IR, it generally neglects to address the relationship of gender to (neo)imperialism and race. (Chowdhry and Nair, 2004, 3)

The allegation directed towards the new imperialism is less that a universalising conception of women and their rights is occluding the aspirations and voices of women of other non-western locations and more that the well-rehearsed debates of feminism in relation to such issues as difference and transnational relations have been appropriated for the racialising project of the War on Terror. Of course, this is not and has never been an absolute distinction. Accounts of earlier phases of imperial feminism have described, for instance, the manner in which campaigns for the empowerment of some women pledged support for the project of empire in order to ally race-privileged women with imperial power and its rewards (McLintock, 1993), or the manner in which the conception of women's empowerment borrowed from racialised ideas about the world (Pratt, 1992) or the ways in which imperial administrations scrutinised, demonised and/or sought to save local women from the clutches of their backward cultures (Spivak, 1988; Mani, 1998). In these accounts of earlier moments, 'race' is a pretty explicit component of the imperial project and allegiance to supremacist models of whiteness is, arguably, a requirement for entry into citizenship. More recent debates have decried the racism of imperial feminism and, after heart-rending battles, most feminists refuse and refute explicit calls to support white-supremacist models of the nation. Women from groups facing racism or social exclusion on the grounds of racial identity may be more inclined to couch their feminism in terms of a racial project, but these tend to be presented as exercises in resistance. Overall, feminism does not sit easily with explicitly racist projects or calls to supremacist solidarity. Instead, feminism has articulated its transnational values in terms of co-operation, human rights, and solidarity between women activists. In this move, there is an attempt to articulate if not a universalist conception of women's rights at least an agreement of shared goals for transnational feminism. In fact, the struggle to articulate goals is itself seen as part of the project of feminism. Suki Ali summarises this point when she writes of global feminism just before the onset of the War on Terror:

The future of feminism is uncertain. Women continue to discuss the meaning of the term and whether they wish to claim the label 'feminist' for themselves or not. There are ongoing debates raging across theoretical boundaries, across geographical and spatial boundaries, and across lines that are marked by shared beliefs. Before we lower our heads in defeat in the face of such disagreement, we should reflect that this is also how the future strength of feminism may be assured. These women who are working full time for and on behalf of women and other oppressed groups still have the energy left to argue and discuss and demand that the women's movement continues to evolve and transform. (Ali, 2000, 3)

The battle over the meaning and centre of feminism has been constitutive of the movement itself in recent times. A movement built through such ongoing and unresolved debate is not easily appropriated by the directive and exclusivist project of nationalism or racist war. However, the model developed through feminism of positing feminist goals as a transnational good validated by the dialogue and agreement of local activists and the adoption of non-universal but strategically essentialist concepts and goals in particular locations appears to have been taken up by proponents of the War on Terror.

In the international arena this means that women's rights can be heralded as the central issue in the invasion and occupation of another state but this event can have no impact on the wider commitment to women's rights in domestic or international arenas. Jacqui Alexander references the work of Charlotte Bunch and Ella Shohat in order to expand this point:

> US feminist mobilizations have provoked transformations in the social relations of gender at the national cultural level but have been less successful in transforming state imperial policy ... opposition to racism, sexism, and homophobia in the United States has never guaranteed the opposition to US global hegemony. (Alexander, 2005, 251)

Although it seems glaringly obvious, it is worth restating here that the claims of ethical foreign policy instantiated as military intervention do not fit easily with aspirations to build sustainable and participatory social institutions. The militarised approach in ethical foreign policy makes sense as an emergency action to stop bad things happening. It offers few clues about how to make good things happen in their place and almost certainly will hamper the creation of co-operative relations with local populations.

To an extent, all these debates are an extension of the ongoing ambivalence that feminists have felt in relation to state power (Lovenduski, 2005). This was regarded as a significant split between the much-derided so-called liberal feminism and other, more radical analyses that argued against attempts to appropriate state power for the cause of women (Rankin and Vickers, 2001). The events of recent years should remind us that even liberal feminists cannot rely on the state alone to achieve justice for women (Stanford Friedman, 2001). Feminism remains a social movement in the deep meaning of that term. Its goals rely on social change that arises from social activism. The freedoms that feminism imagines can come about only through a voluntary change in consciousness throughout society. Coercion may bring some short-term results, but this cannot be the end goal. The power and instruments of states may offer some small defence in desperate times, but the progressive vision of feminism cannot come about if people do not come to this vision freely.

Much of the debate among feminist policy makers and administrators returns to these questions, and the question of the extent to which coercive state power can be deployed usefully for feminist goals remains unanswered. However, all these debates recognise that even the non-violent coercion of resource allocation or political recognition and non-recognition significantly compromise the attainment of consensus in favour of feminist goals. Even when such goals are articulated clearly by local activists, history and power and the role of an interventionary state power complicate the response of other local players.

As a result, feminist activists have sought to create transnational alliances that do not rely on state power and that seek to create social change across borders through co-operation and participation as opposed to any coercive practice. Valentine Moghadam describes the work of transnational feminist networks in these terms:

> Transnational feminisms have devised an organizational structure that consists of active and autonomous local/national women's groups but that transcends localisms or nationalisms ... their discourses are not particularistic but universalistic; they emphasize solidarity and commonality rather than difference. (Moghadam, 2005, 196)

This practice of careful transnational solidarity contrasts starkly with the divisive use of women's rights as a propaganda tool in the War on Terror. In common with many other conflicts, this war is animated by allusions to the welfare of women. Women are being repressed, the (male) enemy desires and hates our women, freedom is embodied in the persons of our emancipated women and this is what is under attack; it is the women who have been denied schooling and a role in public life and they will rebuild their nations. Underlying such stories is the assumption that women are victims, survivors and reconstructors but not combatants. Nordstrom refers to her experience of researching in conflict zones to explain the significance of this construction in understandings of war:

> One iconic representation of women did circulate widely: 'the pregnant women disemboweled by terrorists'. This icon is intended as a call to arms, and appears worldwide. This pregnant woman, always nameless as befits her iconic status, has been killed in every city and country at war I have been in; and although such atrocities do occur, the use of this image as an icon effectively obscures all the many women and girls who die and fight without recognition. (Nordstrom, 2005, 400)

The function of this icon is to reassert the place of women as passive victims of armed conflict, with this victimhood most intensely embodied through the display of reproductive function. As Nordstrom argues, such a focus on the vulnerability of the non-combatant and properly-gendered-because-pregnant woman serves to erase the extent to which women and girls are active participants in war in many ways, including as combatants but more often in other, equally dangerous roles. She goes on to explain further:

> In war, women are serving whether they are in a recognized military unit or not. They carry out primary functions of war, they are central targets, they are tortured and killed in numbers as great as, and often greater than, males . . . and they are generally unarmed. There is a profound irony in this: women in many locales are denied access to military combat positions because, ostensibly, it is too dangerous. This leaves them vulnerable to attack without weapons, training, and backup. My focus rests with a world today where the majority of battle deaths are civilians, and wars rage across community centers, not remote battlefields. In such a world, the unarmed *are* the frontlines. Women at the epicenters of political violence who are not part of a formal military are fighting, uniformed or not. (Nordstrom, 2005, 402)

Such a recognition complicates the narrative of rescue that permeates feminist and human rights accounts of military and other western intervention. Inderpal Grewal suggests that this approach is an unexpected outcome of debates within feminism:

> Whereas earlier forms of 'global feminism' … suggested that all women were 'sisters', the impact of race-based and class-based critiques resulted in the formulation of a multiculturalist diversity, albeit without any conflicts or contradictions. Crucially, therefore, this 'common' framework which incorporated difference constructed 'American' feminist subjects in the United States in particular ways and enabled them to become agents in the practice of 'rescuing' victims of human rights violations. (Grewal, 2005, 153)

It has been widely reported that the lives of women in Afghanistan and Iraq continue to be filled with danger and repression (Sharifzada, 2006; Amnesty International, 2005). Despite the claim of Coalition forces that the anti-woman regime of the Taliban had been defeated, reputable commentators have argued that similar patterns of public terror and religiously informed authoritarianism continue in the post-Taliban era. Those hailed as allies of the West during the current war in Afghanistan now appear to repeat the same offences that enraged western sensibilities, including the brutal repression of women. At the same time, the cultivation of opium has increased again, after a period of Talibanisation that made the drug trade far too dangerous to pursue (UNODC, 2007).

Understandably, western commentators have taken these revelations as another indication that the wars in Afghanistan and Iraq were wrong. Our rulers pretended that military intervention was to improve the lives of women, and yet the lives of women remain desperate with little hope of improvement in the near future. The implication is that, therefore, the wars were wrong because they did not achieve this goal of freeing women. The danger is that this seems to suggest that, if the goal of women's emancipation had been reached, then the wars would be justified. At the same time, allegations about the 'barbaric', 'anti-woman' cultures of minority groups in the West operate to justify everyday War on Terror activity. However unsubstantiated, the suggestion that this war is designed to defend and/or rescue women continues to shape popular responses. The belief that rescue could ever be achieved warps the relations between the West and the rest of the world.

2
Bodies, Fears and Rights

This War on Terror has been characterised by the relentless visibility of women in the portrayal of international conflict, not primarily as combatants, but as the constant reference point in explanations and justifications of the war. Of course, this too is nothing new. The display and discussion of women and their place has formed a central component of all sorts of conflict, from the repressive claims of religious movements (Bhatt, 1997) and fascist parties (Durham, 1998) to nationalist struggles that at once celebrate and constrain the activity of women (De Mel, 2001; Kampworth, 2002) to more formal inter-state conflicts where women are allocated a highly gendered form of citizenship, there has been no lack of visibility for women in conflict situations.

However, I want to suggest that there is something a little different about the narratives of gender that cut through the War on Terror. Somehow women's bodies have become inserted into the central iconography of the War on Terror. This is not the feminised embodiment of earlier conflicts. There is no Britannia figure to embellish war memorabilia or to figure as a call to arms (McKenzie, 1986) Neither is this a conflict that has its own pin-ups. There is no space for forces' darlings in this conflict, because, it seems, that kind of feminine embodiment cannot carry the gravitas of military conflict for us any more. Instead, the War on Terror has circulated a different kind of feminine embodiment. This is a conflict in which there are constant references to the bodies of women and the relation of such embodiment to freedom. What can women wear? Where can they go? How freely can they move? How constrained are they in public space? How comfortable can they be in their own skins? Women's bodies are an underlying referent in so many aspects of this war. Ratna Kapur argues that, in the months following the invasion of Afghanistan, the

46

representation of symbolically 'unveiled' Afghani women served as a visual talisman for the ideological message of this war.

> For several days in the middle of November, the 'liberation' of the women of Afghanistan became headline news. The print media around the Western world flashed pictures of Afghan women, with veils cast aside, smiling for the cameras after the Taliban were forced out of Kabul. The message seemed simple enough – the military intervention in Afghanistan had liberated the Afghan women from the tyrannical rule of the Taliban. (Kapur, 2002)

The literal visibility of women's faces and bodies signalled victory against the dysfunctional and barbaric patriarchal violence of the Taliban – the image of the lifting of veils brings together a critique of religio-political movements and their oppression of women, a portrayal of freedom as embodied in freedom of dress and a re-humanising of the othered woman by restoring her face to public view. Whereas the war on Iraq has been less explicitly linked to ideas about the proper place and appearance of women, Sjoberg argues that in this phase, too, the War on Terror is represented as a series of narratives about the place of women in conflict.

> In the 2003 war in Iraq, Americans saw images of a teenage girl as a war hero, of a female general in charge of a military prison where torture took place, of women who committed those abuses, of male victims of wartime sexual abuse and of the absence of gender in official government reactions to the torture at Abu Ghraib. I contend that several gendered stories from the 2003 war in Iraq demonstrate three major developments in militarized femininity in the United States: increasing sophistication of the ideal image of the woman soldier, stories of militarized femininity constructed in opposition to the gendered enemy and evident tension between popular ideas of femininity and women's agency in violence. (Sjoberg, 2007, 83)

The high profile given to debates about the proper place of women and the focus on roles taken by women have been apparent in the conduct of the military aspects of the War on Terror. I will argue that, in fact, this war extends far beyond recognised zones of conflict and that the struggle over the meaning and place of gender continues in these other arenas. In part this excessive visibility can be seen as an implicit retort to feminist analyses of militarism which critique the masculinist construction of military activity and space. Against this, this is a structure of conflict where women are positioned, displayed and included in very knowing ways. This is not to say that there are not traces of earlier, more familiar gender mythologies. There are still calls for women to be doting mothers, resilient wives, dutiful daughters, all in order to show proper appreciation for the centrality of male fighters and defenders. There are the injunctions for women to play their part in the militarised drama, while keeping to suitably gendered displays of solidarity, as soldiers who are also wives and mothers and daughters. All of these demands have been made before in other conflict situations – from munitions workers (Thom, 2000; Williams, 2002) to nationalist fighters (Kampworth, 2002; Hamilton, 2007) to the frontline soldiers of the 1991 Gulf War who were seen to embody the progressive values of western democracies so advanced that women could be allowed to play a full role in the military (Enloe, 1993).

The militarised incursions of the War on Terror also reference these histories of militarised femininity. These wars also have their patient wives and mothers at home and their plucky girl soldiers in the field. However there is also in this conflict an extension and addition to the deployment of femininity for militarised ends.

This is a conflict that not only purports to defend 'our' womenfolk from the attacks of a barbaric enemy, but that also calls on a conception of feminism and women's rights that demands the visibility of women. If the iconic image of women's repression in this campaign has been the forced veiling of women under the Taliban, then empowerment for women has been conceived and demonstrated through a series of symbolic unveilings. This trope of unveiling has emerged as the favoured representation of a grateful population greeting their liberators (Kapur, 2002), as a marker of entry into the western(ised) public life of commodification (Rodriguez and Ohlson, 2007), as the gesture that confirms the feminised status of the occupied space, once again revealed to invaders in the manner of a woman's body (Hesford and Kozol, 2005) and as the metaphor that indicates the unmasking of the (Muslim) other (Sanoff, 2005).

Within the nations of the coalition (and beyond) this has resulted in an escalating crisis in relation to ethnic diversity, the status of women, and the politics of race (Shore, 2006; Modood et al., 2006). The confusion between international and national levels of threat and the place of Islam in all of this flux has led again to a fixation on the appearance of women. The headscarf and the face veil have taken on an excessively heightened symbolic role as the marker dividing western values of women's freedom (to be uncovered) from Islamic constraints (Thomas, 2006; Scott, 2005; Winter, 2006; Gallala, 2006). Other instances where women (or men) may cover their heads or faces for reasons of religion or fashion have become invisible, while the coverings of Muslim women have become hypervisible and regarded as a confrontational affront to western values. Of course, this whole process must assume as an alternative a mode of public appearance and behaviour that embodies the freedoms enjoyed by western(ised) women.

Consumption, sexualisation and the emancipated western(ised) woman

I want to argue that whereas previous fantasies of imperial femininity relegated western women to a passive role as the feminine ideal safely ensconced in the home (for more complex analyses of this, see Procida, 2002; Whitlock, 2000), this time there is a more active engagement imagined for western women as envoys of a western feminism that characterises freedom in market-friendly terms, including a buy-in to commodified versions of sexual emancipation. While activists from transnational feminist movements may not recognise the account of feminism given in such representations, the suggestion that social movements may reach their goals through the extension of a market that is held in proper balance by the checks of a functioning state is familiar from Walzer's famous work on global civil society (Walzer, 1995). It is a small step from this to representing feminism as taking place through participation in market-based models of democracy-building.

In the manner of other nationalist projects, the cultural articulation of the War on Terror as a war to protect the freedoms of western(ised) women also serves to shape and discipline these same protected women. The barbarian hordes in this conflict are, apparently, intent on imposing their violent anti-women culture on the world and in particular on a debauched and depraved West that has been corroded by the evils of consumer sex and material frippery. Just as there has been an injunction to Muslim minorities in Europe to declare again and again their moderation in belief and repugnance of violence (Choudhury, 2001; Miraj, 2006), there has been a similar if more muted call on women to declare their gratitude and fear.

If the 'us' and 'them' terms of the War on Terror polarise Muslim and other allegiances, they also serve to define how the supposed freedoms of women can be embodied and displayed. Both the horrors of the Taliban and the rhetoric of the US-led coalition seek to construct a seamless association between the veiling of women, the constraint of women's movement and the refusal of women's rights to education and participation in public life. For both sides, the appearance or non-appearance of women's bodies is where it all begins, and therefore the issue of women's status is fought out in battles about clothing codes.

Unfortunately, the accounts of the United Nations and other development agencies remind us that women lack access to education, political rights and other basic freedoms in many places, with and without veils (Womenwatch, 2007). Women's appearance continues to be a problematic choice of symbolic marker, not least because the covering, uncovering and display of women's bodies have been central areas of struggle for feminism (for recent work revisiting these questions, see Tiggemann et al., 2005; Colls, 2004).

My argument is that the display of women's bodies and the manner of their display is a central aspect of the dissemination of the culture and values of the new imperialism, and that the civilisation of the West is being measured by the ability of western/westernised women to embody the concept of rights through the deployment of their own physicality, both in posture and mobility. This shows a melding of discussions of women's rights with ideas of sexual rights and of the ability to exercise sexual agency as an iconic right that comes to symbolise a larger fantasy of what it is to be free (for a nuanced revisiting of these arguments, see Altman, 2001). This particular fantasy bears the characteristics of one approach to human rights – the sanctity of the individual, the holding of rights as a personal treasure, the privileging of choice and the exercise of individual agency – all of them important and wondrous conceptions of human freedom, but limited to one aspect of how freedom might be exercised. As others have commented, the more collective rights of security, fulfilment of basic needs, and freedom from violence and uncertainty do not fall easily into this version of freedom (Krishna, 2007). As rights that are needed but that are not exercised, it is difficult to construct a narrative of personal freedom and agency around these themes. The eroticised character of the one who has the right to do as he or she please is a more seductive and market-friendly incarnation of the attractions of human rights for all. The woman who demonstrates her freedom through physical display, with an implication of sexual autonomy and participation in consumer markets, becomes the favoured incarnation of femininity and an image to elevate above more troublesome models of feminine embodiment.

Mothering, reproduction and terror

Mothers are a favourite theme in cultures of war. Appeals to mother love, motherland, duty, protection, home and hearth and the heart of the nation all revolve around that old trope – that women's citizenship and social status emerge from reproductive relations. It is predictable, then, that the War on Terror has its own recurring narrative of mothering. I have argued that this war represents, among other things, the deployment of women, feminism and femininity in a battle against and about men and the attempted creation of a global public space of alliance against terrorism. I want to suggest that the development of this global arena – however contested – is a central aspect of the War on Terror. Of course, in some ways this is obviously the case. We know only too well that the battle is between 'us' and 'them', that it is a battle of 'cultures and values', that what is under attack is our very way of life, and the constant repetition of these themes confirms that the assertion of a shared identity is an important aspect of this whole endeavour. Representations of mothering play an important role in this work.

This book has argued that the War on Terror attempts to construct a global public through a series of overlapping means: a reclaiming of dirty warfare as a necessary evil in the defence of democracy (or our way of life etcetera), an attempted rewriting of the proper jurisdiction of international law (with implications for the terms of consensus around legality within national spaces), and an aspiration to create a global audience and polity that participates in 'our' way of life as distinct elements in the larger conception of global public.

The three elements reinforce each other and aspects of each are wheeled out as justification for another. For example, War on Terror detainees are seen to be denied legal rights because they do not participate in our way of life and therefore, it is alleged, fall outside the contract of legality. Dirty warfare is necessary because we are dealing with people who do not understand the values of human rights and respect for life and therefore we must institute a barbarism than can match theirs. These manoeuvres rely on a widespread acceptance of the proposed terms of our way of life, even from those who oppose military intervention or the erosion of civil liberties. This is a construction that serves to enrol dissenters into group membership and to consolidate the sense of a coherent and shared identity that can be seen as 'us', with diversity within this term serving as yet another proof of the benefits of our values.

My interest is in how we are positioned to take up this role and through what means. There are a range of themes in this process – but gendering bubbles through most of them. The intensive cultural work that we are all experiencing impacts, inevitably, on how the most visible and powerful mythologies of gendering appear in various fora of public culture. Here I want to consider some high-profile examples and to consider the representation of mothers, parenting, and what it is to be a man.

The extremist mother

One theme that circulates in popular discussions of terrorism is the role of the (extremist) mother. In Britain, government has adopted a highly contentious strategy of addressing Muslim women and mothers as those who are best placed to challenge extremism and radicalisation (UK Department for Communities and Local Government, 2008). Underlying such initiatives, other more sensationalist accounts can be discerned. Who raises sons (and now daughters) to carry out such atrocities? What kind of mothering allows such disregard for human life? What has gone wrong in the journey of human nurture, because only a failure of nurture could produce monsters with no empathy for the victims of their violence?

The resurgent interest in the (of course not new) phenomenon of international terrorism has given rise to a range of accounts of how such horror can happen, both from established political and scholarly commentators and from amateur analysts of all colours (Booth and Dunne, 2002; Ankersen, 2007; Laqueur, 1999). In common with public commentary on other causes of fear such as knife and gun crime, this discussion has included considerable speculation about the factors that contribute to the psychological make-up of a terrorist (Frost, 2005; Taylor and Horgan, 2006; Schmidt, Joffe and Davar, 2005).

For some, this is no mystery. The highly partisan website Palestinian Media Watch (http://www.pmw.org.il) compiles a catalogue of the Palestinian mothers of alleged suicide bombers, accompanied by attributed quotations that glorify terrorism and that conflate motherly love and filial duty with celebrations of violence. Israeli propaganda has circulated this view for some time, as a component of the Israeli view that there can be no negotiation with Palestinians because these barbarians are immune to reason (Bhattacharyya, 2008). The suggestion that some cultures glorify violence and destruction, including self-destruction, for their own sake and in preference to the values of love, protection and nurture between parents and children, casts terrorist violence as a kind of psychological disorder arising from failures of culture and parenting. In the War on Terror, these allegations have been taken beyond Palestinians and are presented as a global weakness of Islam. The implication is that 'we', participants in humane and western-inspired values, have learned the importance of affective family relations in the creation of balanced citizens, unlike these others who neglect their children and their parental duty and sacrifice their offspring to faceless causes that do not recognise individual worth.

It is hard not to rise to this bait. Look all over the world, violence is not limited to any one community. Plenty of the sons and daughters of the West display equal if not greater thirst for blood and disregard for the human consequences of their actions (Global Policy Forum, 2007). One strand in the literature suggests that high-tech warfare is designed to enhance and utilise this sense of disengagement from those on the receiving end of military attacks (Hirst, 2001; Hables Gray, 1997). Equally we can point to the numerous documented instances of excessive and seemingly sadistic violence carried out by coalition forces when they do meet others face to face (Taguba, 2004; Aitken, 2008).

However, I am not sure that these competing claims of barbarity address the heart of the matter. If anything, the setting up of the debate as a set of competing claims between the terrorism of states and of non-states is itself an element of the creation of the public space of grudging assent that I am identifying.

Therefore, instead of another battle over who is more barbaric, or whether dangerous times call for desperate measures, I want to consider the depiction of mothering in three key tropes – not all new –

but all adapted for use in the cultural work of the Global War on Terror.

Suicide bombing

The most heated and extensive discussion has been in relation to the personal formation of suicide bombers. In an echo of earlier mythologies of the mothers of a military enemy, the War on Terror has been characterised by a fixation on suicide bombing as the emblematic terror act. This particular tactic has been taken as an indication of the absolute difference between 'us' and 'them', and this instance of the boundary is seen to stem from the dysfunctional subject formation of so-called enemies of the West. Of course, such disturbed behaviour must stem from questionable mothering.

The media interest in Mariam Farahat is a key example. Farahat ran as a Hamas candidate in the 2006 Gaza election. This is one media account of her notoriety:

> In Gaza, Farahat is known as Um Nidal, or Mother of the Struggle – a mother who sent three of her six sons on Hamas suicide missions against Israeli targets.
>
> 'We consider it holy duty,' she told ABC News. 'Our land is occupied. You take all the means to banish the occupier. I sacrificed my children for this holy, patriotic duty. I love my children, but as Muslims we pressure ourselves and sacrifice our emotions for the interest of the homeland. The greater interest takes precedence to the personal interest.'
>
> She is most famous for being in a Hamas video that showed her seventeen-year-old how to attack Israelis and told him not to return. Shortly afterward, he killed five students in a Jewish settlement before being killed himself. Um Nidal's home has become a shrine to her dead sons, with admirers and other members of Hamas often dropping by. (ABC News, 2006)

The key components of this myth are also those demonstrated on the Palestinian Media Watch website. In recent years, this narrative has moved beyond Israeli accounts of supposed Palestinian barbarity and has entered a larger global narrative about the boundaries of civilisation. In this more recent telling, the pathology of the Islamic other is presented as a counterpoint to the most celebrated and admirable values of the West (Bhattacharyya, 2008).

The most obvious allegation is that this violence arises from a perversion of motherly love that has failed to raise, nurture and protect and instead abandoned nurture in favour of destruction.

The perverse cultures that allow this warped articulation of parent–child love are alleged to have abandoned the proper goals of child rearing. Instead of appreciating the unique individuality of the child and the responsibility of the parent to nurture that child in an inward-looking and insistently non-collective vision of affective development, the mothers of suicide bombers are presented as having become ciphers for a larger and depersonalised battle, refusing the claims of intimate relations and instead viewing children as contributions to some other struggle beyond the family.

At the heart of this depiction of perverse parenting is the suggestion that there is a heartless call on the affective claims of parenthood. These are monsters that not only raise their children to become human sacrifices, they incite such violence in all children in the name of love for their mother, as a demonstration of the devotion of an obedient and loving child.

The internet provides endless opportunities to expound on such theories of cultural difference. The psychohistory project of Lloyd deMause is one example that brings together a number of our key themes. Although I do not wish to present deMause as an authoritative source, I do want to argue that the manner of his argument is illustrative of one aspect of War on Terror culture. DeMause seeks to explain international conflict and turbulence between nations through the lens of individual psychology. In pursuit of this project, he publishes an online book, The Emotional Life of Nations, and includes a chapter entitled 'The Childhood Origins of Terrorism' (www.psychohistory.com/htm/eln03_terrorism.html). Here deMause parades a series of key narrative moments in the mythology of the pathologically terrorist-raising culture. The battle against liberal western values arises from the backward child-rearing practices of non-western spaces. As a result, deMause argues, 'It would be useful to know what makes a terrorist – what development-mental life histories they share that can help us see why they want to kill 'American infidels' and themselves – so we can apply our efforts to removing the sources of their violence' (deMause, 2002, 1). This injunction moves on from the condemnation of inexplicable evil that characterises some depictions of terrorism. However, political or historical analyses are disallowed here too. The key to understanding can be found 'not in this or that American foreign policy error but in the extremely abusive families of terrorists' (deMause, 2002, 1). The root of this violence is argued to lie in the personal psychological distress of the individual, a distress that stems from the interpersonal disturbance of the family, not any larger dissatisfaction. This fixation on the troubled childhoods of alleged terrorists appears to resonate with wider psychologisation and individualisation of social understanding in the popular domain, as if terrorism too could be compartmentalised into the scrutinising box of reality television, celebrity culture and abuse paperbacks that present survivor testimony as both entertainment and spiritual enlightenment. The suggestion that anti-social behaviour stems from family dysfunction speaks to the preoccupation of western/ised societies with personal autonomy, the fantasy of the perfectibility of the individual life and the sense that the truth of social pathology can be understood only through attention to the personal affective journey of the individual. In the explanatory narrative of what makes a terrorist, this approach utilises a series of key touchstones in order to plot the story. First there is the allegation that these are products of a misogynist system. This leads to abuse of girls and women in both public and private spheres of life – 'it is not surprising that these mutilated, battered women make less than ideal mothers, reinflicting their own miseries upon their children' (deMause, 2002, 2). This culture of abuse leads to widespread physical and sexual abuse of children with excessive levels of punishment. As a result, abused children grow up conflicted and unable to reconcile their desire for western/ised freedoms, including most importantly the desire for sexual freedom, with the need for maternal approval; the resulting rage spills out into violence. The account constructed by deMause may appear to be inflammatory and extreme, but its key elements are echoed in a range of more carefully worded material (Buruma and Margalit, 2004; for a more careful review of similar ideas, see Choudhury, 2007).

These speculations about the cultural antecedents of terrorism represent a particular and highly significant strategy of othering. This is a narrative that accounts for political violence by relegating political differences and conflict to symptoms of family dysfunction – another indication of how less than human these people are, and proof that the affective relations of such people are worth nothing and that death is no cause of grief for them. Within this account, the status of women and attitudes to sexuality play a central role in the narrative. These are identified as the root of terrorist culture, because it is through these means that dysfunctional families create unhappy individuals filled with violent hatred and rage, apparently.

Radicalisation

The story of authoritarian abuse is accompanied by another distinct but strangely complementary account of parental culpability. In this parallel narrative, it is too-lax parenting that leads to terror. The commentary surrounding the so-called American Taliban, John Walker Lindh, exemplifies this trend.

> The question that obsessed them all was what could have turned a smart kid from a well-to-do background in suburban California into an Islamist extremist, fighting for his country's sworn enemy in Afghanistan.
>
> The answer most people found was two-fold, or rather, two sides of the same coin: the faddism of 'Bay Area culture' and excessively liberal parenting.
>
> Ronald Kuby, the lawyer who coincidentally represented the 1993 World Trade Center bombers, summed up the case for the prosecution when he described Lindh as 'a pathetic schlub who was deluded by religion and badly in need of parental guidance'. So Frank Lindh and (his estranged wife) Marilyn Walker stood condemned: their permissive parenting had raised an authentic American anti-hero. (Seaton, 2002)

There are two familiar themes here. One is a reworking of an old complaint against liberal parenting as too permissive, too coddling, the opposite of suicide-bomber mothering and yet equally dangerous. Liberal parenting creates social monsters, so the complaint goes, because children learn no values and boundaries (Shaw, 2003) and in their search for anti-authoritarian stances that can re-establish the (apparently necessary) boundary between child and parent, the off-spring of liberal parents are forced to adopt more and more extreme and outlandish positions – until they join the Taliban!

A variation on this theme is the suggestion that young men join terrorist groups because their parents cannot offer sufficient and sufficiently constant attention. In some tellings this is a result of external pressures, as in the relatively sympathetic portrayal of the mother of Zacaria Massoui, a 9/11 suspect, as a hard-working single mother whose arduous cleaning job limited her time with her family.

In others, the allegation adapts older racialised mythologies of absent fathers and overbearing mothers. Analysis of the pathologisation of African-American families has been central to accounts of both the deep psychic disturbance of racism in American society and the manner in which such fantasies of race and sexuality can come to shape serious policy discussion and the material outcomes of everyday life (Spillers, 1987; Neubeck and Cazanave, 2001). There have been similar debates in British public culture, although increasingly the allegation has been that this socially dangerous parenting comes from the new racialised category of the antisocial family (Garrett, 2007).

The racialised demonisation of disadvantaged family life now brings together a number of overlapping mythologies. The longstanding pathologisation of black communities coincides with an accompanying Orientalist depiction of the supposedly deficient structure of the black family. The reworking of the idea of the underclass as a socially disruptive cultural corrosive combines with depictions of some cultures, such as Islam or other cultures of minority migrants to the West, as destructively authoritarian and/or distantly impersonal and unable to build the successful affective relations that make families and good citizens. All strands lead back to the main allegation – bad parents with inadequate cultures make sick men.

Guantánamo – the spectacle of the open secret

The processes that I am gathering here under the term 'embodiment' include narratives about how bodies come to be and take meaning; representations of bodies varyingly uniformed and undressed, constrained or contorted; and the integration of iconic glimpses and rumours into a kind of propaganda of suggestion that creates an understanding of how bodies may be treated, circulated and interpreted without ever stating these as explicit injunctions.

The illegal prison at Guantánamo Bay has served as an important element of this process of suggestion. The acknowledgement of Guantánamo's existence and purpose has formed part of the official account of the War on Terror. Unlike earlier dirty wars, this is not a secret prison, although we have come to learn that it represents the visible tip of a hidden mass of secret prisons (Grey, 2006). Instead of a secret, this is a crime shrouded in euphemism. It is Guantánamo and its associated activities that have introduced the world to key terms of the War on Terror. Now we understand such phrases as 'detention facility' and 'enemy combatant', tacitly accepting the US account of rights and laws through their use. The battle about the jurisdiction of the Geneva Convention has been played out in public, and, despite the challenges to this view, has served to reaffirm the suggestion that there may be some who fall outside such agreements (for reviews of these debates see Johns, 2005; Steyn, 2004; Murphy, 2003). The open existence of Guantánamo serves as an affirmation of the practices of kidnapping your enemies from ill-defined fields of battle, of transporting them thousands of miles across the world, of the use of such tactics as hooding and shackling in transit and of the use of highly punitive forms of imprisonment as an aspect of warfare. All of these things are highly contested and represent a significant distortion of previously accepted rules governing the conduct of war (Sands, 2005; Booth and Dunne, 2002). Guantánamo fulfils the requirements of neither prisoner-of-war camp nor penal institution. Prisoners there are punished but not allowed the protections of criminal proceedings. They are identified as enemy fighters but not accorded the privileges of prisoners of war. That this ambiguity is openly proclaimed as a necessary development for new circumstances forms part of the suggestive framework I am seeking to identify.

From the outset Guantánamo has given the world some of the most iconic and widely circulated images of the War on Terror. Reviewing the visual presentation of the prison, it is hard not to surmise that this was the intention. Images of hooded and shackled prisoners kneeling in their jumpsuits behind wire fencing and under the watch of armed guards were disseminated almost immediately. Other early and iconic images showed shackled and jumpsuited prisoners being stretchered to interrogation by armed guards. Both images were authorised by US military. Revealing these images, but little more, creates an imaginary space in which a global public can surmise what may occur but cannot verify through official sources. The official account tells the world that these are bad men to be hooded, shackled, interrogated in a physically onerous manner and that such practices are no secret and no shame. However it leaves open to the imagination what else is authorised in this legal black hole. The world sees enough to learn to be terrified at what we do not see.

Visualisation and embodiment

It has been the revelations of images from Abu Ghraib that have fuelled public debate about what can be seen in the War on Terror. Before this there had been little consideration of the visual incarnation of 'enemies' or of the theatrical display of such an unlimited war. In the initial conception of 'us' and 'them', the 'axis of evil' and the supposedly new threat of international terrorism both enemy and military tactics remained largely invisible. Apart from the iconic images of Bin Laden, this was a faceless enemy, a hidden army harboured, encouraged and perhaps financed by this evil axis of states but sufficiently invisible to blend into western societies without remark. The media coverage of the invasion of Afghanistan showed preparation but little else; we were told that this war was 'won' by aerial bombardment but the visual relaying of this to the rest of the world was at this point not yet a component of the campaign.

It is not until the explicit celebration of 'shock and awe' aerial bombardment as an integral aspect of the invasion of Iraq that there is an open acknowledgement of the role of the visual in this larger global war. 'Shock and awe' was a version of military display designed not only for the unlucky recipients of such intensive bombing but also for the global media transmitting the progress of the war to diverse audiences across the world. Eighteen months into this 'war against evil', the US clearly believed that it was necessary and useful to reaffirm the absolute might and dominance of their military machine in the manner most suited to media transmission. This was before the world had grown weary of the nightly images of carnage on Iraqi streets and was a display that combined the methods of techno-war in that the fireworks were designed to show the technological might of a power that could conduct war cleanly and from afar with a resurrection of less fashionable assertions of power. Alan Feldman identifies this moment as a particular shift in US military and media strategy.

> Since the first day of 'shock and awe', visual violence and visual dominance has guided American military strategy in Iraq. This was a war whose main objective was to make elusive terrorists and their hidden weapons *visible*, a war that sought to reduce an elusive transnational cell structure to a fixed national location, to fashion an identifiable and stable object of American retribution. Making elusive others visible and

demonstrating control through advanced optical technology – from the Iraqi 'theatre' to the American living-room – was a central political tenet of this mediatised war. (Feldman, 2004)

Feldman is not speaking of the circulation of racialised rumour or images of abuse. However his arguments about the centrality of the visual to this war should be noted. The idea that the objective has been to create an identifiable object of retribution helps us to make sense of the insistent visualisation of abuse and the widespread circulation of rumours of absolute and impossible difference between so-called civilizations and the alleged necessity of shocking violence.

Not all commentators have agreed that the circulation of visual images constitutes part of the battle plan of the War on Terror. In her commentary on the Abu Ghraib photographs, Hazel Carby argues against this that it is the endless visibility of these photographs that has the most severe impact for the United States government:

> The most severe impact of Abu Ghraib for the United States government has been the fact that the actions there of its military personnel and civilian contractors have been seen across the world. The dissemination of images by western and Arab media, including the internet, meant that the scandal, as well as being seen as a legal violation and moral outrage, was played and replayed in the hearts and minds of citizens in every country. (Carby, 2004)

Carby argues that the staging and circulation of the Abu Ghraib photographs is based on the genre of lynching photographs, serving not only to consolidate the white community's sense of united supremacism, but also to resurrect this spectre of racial terror. These mementoes of vicious racist violence were designed to corral whites into complicity through shared spectatorship (Allen et al., 2000). Dissent would be betrayal of the community gathered around the battered and burnt black body. Looking served as a marker of participation and collaboration. At the same time, the lynching photograph served as a warning to black people that this was the fate that awaited any who challenged the privileges of white supremacism. Carby argues that it is damaging to the US for this dynamic to be revealed again in images from Iraq. Undoubtedly for many the circulation of such images confirms their existing beliefs about the United States. Much of the world needs little convincing of American brutality or of the idea that US intervention is motivated by US self-interest as opposed to any more high-minded motives (for accounts of

US-sponsored torture see Harbury, 2005; Otterman, 2007). For them, these revelations were enraging but not surprising. Not only in the light of other bloody US interventions but also through an understanding of the War on Terror influenced by the propaganda of suggestion, Abu Ghraib only extended the implications of the snippets from Guantánamo and the rumours from Baghram. In the manner of horror-film audiences, much of the world expected there to be this horror behind the door. The sense of scandal arose from the stark hypocrisy of terming the Iraq war and occupation a 'humanitarian intervention' and, in relation to this, the photographs have come to be iconic of the discomforts of this war for western/ised audiences.

As an example, Susan Sontag wrote an influential and widely cited comment piece on the implications of the photographs in which she summarises thus:

> The issue is not whether a majority or a minority of Americans performs such acts but whether the nature of the policies prosecuted by this administration and the hierarchies deployed to carry them out makes such acts likely. ... Considered in this light, the photographs are us. That is, they are representative of the fundamental corruptions of any foreign occupation together with the Bush administration's distinctive policies. (Sontag, 2004)

Of course, such a statement is of high rhetorical importance. Sontag's earlier work on photography popularised the semiotic analysis of photographs and questioned the claim of the technology to provide representations of the real. For this reason it is of particular significance that she argues for the representative status of these photographs, not because this is a direct representation of the actions of the majority of the population but because such images take on a representative function in the context of military occupation coupled with a stated intention to dismantle the framework of international law. Sontag identifies two other key aspects of the Abu Ghraib scandal; that these were images created for the express purpose of dissemination and that we live in an age when the proliferation of such images is unstoppable:

> The lynching pictures were in the nature of photographs as trophies – taken by a photographer in order to be collected, stored in albums, displayed. The pictures taken by American soldiers in Abu Ghraib, however, reflect a shift in the use made of pictures – less objects to be saved than messages to be disseminated, circulated. (Sontag, 2004)

And even if our leaders choose not to look at them, there will be thousands more snapshots and videos. Unstoppable. (Sontag, 2004)

The Abu Ghraib images replay key themes from other colonial settings. However horrible, there is little here to surprise anyone familiar with the racialised violence of other occupations (Rao, 2001; Lazreg, 2007). Equally the repetitive playing out of sexual abuse and humiliation is not a new theme. The known histories of torture show that rape, sexual abuse and pain directed at sexual organs have been central to the conduct of other terror campaigns (for an example, see Otterman, 2007). For those who have been willing to listen, similar revelations have emerged from US-sponsored torture camps through the Cold War and from the even more impenetrable dungeons of non-aligned dictatorships of recent decades (Harbury, 2005; Otterman, 2007). Yet despite these well-known phenomena, a key aspect of response to the Abu Ghraib images has been a vociferous assertion that these constitute the most disgusting and *unimaginable* of revelations. I want to argue that there is a particular kind of work done by the excessive displays of outrage at the photographs from Abu Ghraib, most significantly when the outraged party wishes to defend the wider project of the War on Terror by demonstrating their outrage at such an aberration (for a commentary on this see Foley, 2004).

Such expressions serve to reaffirm that 'we' do not do such things, otherwise it would not be so shocking, and that we have not done such things in the past (although there is ample evidence that we have). Theatricalised disgust also confirms that this is depravity, not security strategy, and that these images reveal a horror beyond imagination, certainly far beyond the respectable conduct of this justifiable and humanitarian war. The tortured and dead beyond these images are erased from discussion. These images also serve to confirm the propaganda of suggestion by asserting that the abuses that are surmised from the almost-information of official representations are the product of over-fevered imaginations. As a result, a global public continues to fear that the worst may be happening but lacks the means to verify its worst fears.

Human rights and military intervention

The War on Terror brings together a conceptualisation of war and of the duty/right to intervene militarily that has emerged over a number of years as an implicit critique of the norms of international law. This apparent tension between the rights of the sovereign state and the responsibility of the international community to safeguard human rights everywhere has been regarded as a central question in global governance. Some have argued that such an apparent championing of human rights as defined by non-governmental organisations (NGOs) above any claims made by elected representatives within countries is a thin veil for the reassertion of the right of powerful states to intervene wherever they choose (Chandler, 2006; Bricmont, 2006), while others have presented the limits of international law as an indication that powerful nations must reassess their own international role and obligations (Ignatieff, 2003; Kaldor, 1999).

The well-known account of this developing body of ideas gives the desperate failure of the world to intervene to assist victims of the Rwandan genocide and massacres in Bosnia as the trigger event to change (for critical evaluations of this account see Shawcross, 2000; Kuperman, 2001). This is the appeal made by proponents of military intervention in the name of human rights: not to intervene is to allow the possibility of genocide. Such an appeal rests on the belief that the claim of human rights as conceived by powerful nations in conjunction with NGO advisers is greater necessarily than the claims of state sovereignty. It is not a difficult argument for most people – saving lives is more important than diplomatic niceties. Such an emerging consensus appears to have enabled NATO intervention in Kosovo (Chandler, 2006).

The War on Terror builds on this gradual development of an agreement among some powerful nations that military intervention can and must be initiated in defence of human rights and above any legalistic barriers that are erected by formalised relations between states. This current endless war is not quite a war for human rights in the manner of Kosovo. However, the underlying claim that it is always justifiable to employ military force in the defence of human dignity reverberates through the rhetoric of the War on Terror. This may not be an intervention or even a set of interventions against possible genocide, but it is a broad-ranging set of actions to defend 'our' values and way of life. Thus military intervention in Afghanistan frees women from the barbarism of the Taliban, intervention in Iraq deposes the authoritarian brutality of the Ba'athist regime, indefinite detention of so-called enemy combatants is justified because these people seek to bring their inhuman cruelty and indifference to human dignity to our societies, the rule of law everywhere becomes subservient to the greater imperative to defend our values. The issue of torture is central to the claims of the War on Terror not because this is the first or only war where torture has occurred but because the conduct of this war relies on an appeal to human rights to legitimise the overturning of previous norms of inter-state behaviour.

Ariel Dorfman reminds us that 'every regime that tortures does so in the name of salvation' (Dorfman, 2004, 16). Proponents of the War on Terror, however, both do this and promote the idea that if they or their forces commit human rights abuses they are not subject to the processes of law. For these people there is no right to a fair trial or claim of sovereignty, because the horror of their enemies' actions demands that the international community intervenes against them in urgent, pre-emptive and unhampered ways. This argument has come to shape both the conduct of international relations and the practice of domestic law, as will be discussed in the next chapter.

The intensive visualisation of abuse therefore becomes an important part of the battle over what is permissible and who is protected. The exchange of images of violence supplements the ongoing and actual violent exchanges across the world. I do not mean to suggest that this traffic in images is one-way. The parading of prisoners and the transmission of this display via international media have developed to become a stock tactic, most of all for 'enemies of the West'. A central image and scandal of the 1991 Gulf War was the media spectacle of western hostages used in the propaganda tableaux of Saddam Hussein. More recently, hostages taken in Iraq and Afghanistan have been displayed in demeaning poses via the internet and other media, sometimes forced to recite scripted denunciations of their own nations and governments or to beg for help.

If we chart the developing iconography of the War on Terror and the active staging of events as images to be replayed, key moments are presented as attacks on the West. The theatrical destruction of the Twin Towers, the videotapes of Bin Laden flickering across the world's TV and computer monitors, and the horrors of hostage broadcasts including the horrific development of killings transmitted over the internet all reveal an impulse to extend the range and extent of terror through the dissemination of such images.

Of course, such broadcasts have multiple audiences and can serve both to terrorise the self-styled western imagination and to excite and encourage equally self-styled enemies of the West. Both possibilities rely on the ubiquity of media consciousness and the knowledge that a suitably provocative image will be circulated by both mainstream and underground media in a manner that will ensure its place in popular consciousness. These have become the public images of this war. However, at the same time, other, highly suggestive images have been circulated through less mainstream media outlets, and these, too, form part of the open secret of what this war entails.

Embodying danger and masculinity

There is nothing new or surprising about the insistent and repetitive display of idealised masculinities in times of war. Cultural analyses of military conflict have mined this phenomenon extensively and the accompanying accounts of the importance of myths of gender, hetero-sexuality and reproductive relations have informed subsequent under-standings of the cultural business of war (Enloe, 2000; Pettman, 1996; Jacobs and Jacobson, 2000). However, despite all of this boring predictability, I want to consider the particular incarnations of masculinity that emerge in the War on Terror. My point here is not to suggest that this is the first time that masculine types have been created and circulated as part of a war mobilisation or even that this war is more invested in such myths of gendering than others. Instead my interest is in the circulation of masculine types as another key component in the creation of a global public space.

In this I am informed by the work of Klaus Theweleit. This ground-breaking analysis of the role of fantasies of masculinity in the constitution of fighting forces reveals the centrality of obvious and unsubtle displays of phallic prowess.

Theweleit is fortunate in his access to detailed and extensive records and his work is recognised as important both for its analysis and for the uncovering of this mine of data. In our time it seems that there are no such secrets to uncover. Everything is out in the open already, digitally recorded, transmitted via the internet. The fighting forces of the coalition are extensively represented in alternative media. Despite the tight management of official media accounts of the occupation of Iraq and Afghanistan, blogs and webcasts ensure that there is an ongoing stream of images and comment from the ground.

Theweleit's work is engaged in the very particular project of uncovering the formation of the fascist subject in inter-war Germany. In common with others, he presents this as an urgent contemporary political question, for how are we to defeat the seductions of contemporary fascist tendencies unless we understand their lure (Laqueur, 1996)? His analysis of diaries and novels is shaped by a certainty that these people are fascists. The role of Freikorps members in the emergence of the Nazi Party confirms this sense that these artefacts are the work of Nazis in the making.

My suggestion is not that there is an equivalence between any party in the War on Terror and the Freikorps. However, there is something reminiscent of Theweleit's Freikorps material in the constant web broadcasts from Iraq and Afghanistan. Although more often recorded via camera-phone and without the narrative crescendos of written diary/novel forms, this proliferation of representations of the everyday experience of being a combatant creates a body of material that gives insight into the subjectivity of the War on Terror occupying force.

The example that I have been interested in is the website www.liveleak.com. This site accepts freelance footage and includes hundreds if not thousands of amateur video clips from forces in Iraq and Afghanistan. Each day dozens of new clips are uploaded, both from Coalition forces and from other sources. A selection of titles from one week gives an indication of the range and type of contribution, so that we, the public, are invited to watch flash-bang fight sequences: 'Rockets launched from Heli's guided by a laser on insurgents hideout in Iraq' (26/10/07); 'Marines in fire fight with insurgents in truck near Ramadi' (26/10/07); 'Iraq 2/7th platoon calling in 500lb laser guided bomb on insurgents' (21/10/07); 'CH-53 Delta crew – Iraq', showing 'a little bit of the dirty delta experience' (21/10/07). We see military equipment used for sport: 'US soldiers blowing up a tanker by a 203 launcher in North Baji – Iraq' – are 'just another IED attack except this time they had to blow up the tanker to keep the damn locals from stealing the fuel' (26/10/07); 'Bradley vs. car in Ramadi' with footage of a tank crushing a car to a soundtrack of troop laughter (23/10/07). There are complaints too: 'Sand storm during the day at least once a week, I hate this country' (21/10/07).

Footage of the casual abuse of Iraqi children is a notable sub-genre among the submissions: 'Words for food – Iraq' where we learn 'we got this kid to say some dirty words for food' (26/10/07); and 'Push-ups for candy – Iraq' (26/10/07) with a soundtrack of a soldier swearing and abusing children as he orders them to get down and do press-ups for him. This is a small selection from only a few days. There is an overwhelming volume of material, including some with such titles as 'Iraqi caliphate propaganda video' (19/10/07) which shows heroic attacks against Coalition forces to a soundtrack of uplifting Middle Eastern music. There are official films among the clips and excerpts from mainstream media – but it is hard to chart any pattern across such a large and ever-changing body of material. The overall impression is of a relentless will to represent.

One aspect of the echo of the Freikorps material is the insistence of the representational process. So much, so much detail, so much repetition. The recordings of serving forces in Iraq and Afghanistan appear to be relentless, a form of activity for the sake of activity as described by Theweleit. In relation to the Freikorps, Theweleit argues that the process of writing, of filling tightly bound books with tightly bound writing, is itself an important process of consolidating what he calls 'the body-armor'. According to the concept of work used by Theweleit, these men continue such relentless activity in order to stave off the ever-present danger of disintegration. For Theweleit, this is a central aspect of the fascist male, a need to create the self as an impenetrable and upright body untroubled by division, desire or doubt.

It is not necessary to attribute fascist personality or function to forces occupying Iraq and Afghanistan in order to suggest that a similar desire to blot out dissonance may encourage the flow of representations. The rapid and seemingly endless uploading for web broadcast of recordings of forces' life appears to be a response to this need.

Some of the most watched elements of this material offer no narrative or context. This material is not any concerted attempt to correct or even augment the official version of the war or to critique the workings of the war machine. While there is a move towards this mobilisation of military personnel and military families as an anti-war force, only a small number are engaged in mainstream anti-war activism. Whatever the importance of these political initiatives, the great torrents of material coming from serving forces are not of this character. Instead this is commentary by fragment, a series of often indistinguishable clips of explosions, or more often of panicked and excited voiceover followed by explosions, or of an assortment of explosions set to frenetic guitar music (a self-consciously 'white' cultural expression) or commercial rap (now apparently a deracialised demonstration of masculine attitude).

These varied and largely anonymous texts expand the visual iconography of the War on Terror beyond the repeated images of, say, Abu Ghraib to indicate a more diffuse and mundane sexualisation of violence punctuating the boredom of service life. Unlike the torture images and narratives, these clips are, on the whole, sexualised but not explicitly sexual. They are exciting and elicit that physical rush from the viewer that comes with the combination of driving music and fast-paced chase scenes culminating in the climax of release through explosion. However, there are few bodies in these scenes. If the local population appears, it is as distant figures in a form of macabre target practice or as hapless recipients of beatings in reprisal for some imagined infraction.

The sexualisation is shown in part through the construction of the representation – the rhythm and choice of clip, the coupling with a certain style of backing music, the inclusion of the gasping narrative of anticipation and the whooping exclamation when 'targets' are hit. Sometimes we hear young men's voices sharing their delight in the achievement of such a large bang with companions. The overall impression is of both the ongoing horror of being under constant threat of attack and the childish triviality of reducing combat to a game. The ugly playfulness of the images from Abu Ghraib appears less unexpected when read against this more general confusion of sexuality, violence and entertainment. Theweleit identifies a similarly repetitive playing out of sexualised diversions in his material:

> the soldiers' sexuality is not structured in such a way as to allow it to play itself out between persons: it appears capable only of being directed *against* persons, or of realizing itself in one of the various states of oblivion encountered above [shooting, beating, hunting, drinking]. (Theweleit, 1989, 61)

The construction of groups of men into fighting forces has been regarded as, perhaps, the homosocial project *par excellence* (for an example see Zeeland, 1995). The binding of individuals into a group identity that merges the boundaries of personal identity into the welfare of the group has been described as a process combining fear and desire (Bourke, 1999). This, it has been suggested, is one reason why acceptance of women and gay men has been so contentious for the military (Enloe, 1993).

I want to argue that the admission of women or the acknowledgement of the presence of gay and bisexual men need not substantially alter the dynamic of these homosocial processes. Although the classic accounts of the exchange of women and the theatrical demonstration of relations between men posit this process as central to the creation and continuation of patriarchal culture (Rubin, 1975), such practices translate relatively easily into the maintenance of other forms of brutal and exclusive power. Theweleit argues that 'terms such as hetero- or homosexual' (61) cannot be applied usefully to the men whom he studies, because sexuality takes on a different role in the relations and constitution of this group: 'These men seem less to possess a sexuality than to persecute sexuality itself – one way or another' (Theweleit, 1989, 61).

Similarly, the search for identifiable sexual acts and identities in the self-expressions of War on Terror forces is unlikely to be illuminating. Instead it is participation in the persecution of sexuality that appears to ensure entry to the group. Women engaged in recorded abuse of prisoners are required not to display some essence of feminine desire in order to reveal Islam's allegedly pathological fear of female sexuality, but to engage in a shared theatrical display of the excision of sexuality as inter-human relations and its replacement with a persecution of sexuality as a proof of group power.

In his account, Theweleit links the perversion and displacement of sexuality among soldiers to a wider sexualisation of politics in fascist culture. In common with some other commentaries on authoritarian movements, he blurs the distinction between the precise historical period of the Third Reich's ascendance and the ongoing threat that fascistic tendencies exert in our time, in both political address and popular response. It is no longer fashionable to compare consumer capitalism and fascist regimes and that is not my intention here. However, despite his differing focus, Theweleit does identify some other elements of fascist culture that resonate with the cultural expression of the War on Terror. Of course, such claims are difficult to prove – and do not really lie in the realm of proofs. However, those attentive to the cultural formations arising from the War on Terror may recognise something familiar in Theweleit's account of populist politics.

The argument is that political rhetoric operates on a bodily level, not only through the explicit message of the words but also through sexual excitation:

> connoisseurs of the people's flesh conjure up their visions of diverse 'causes for anxiety', they appear credible precisely because their references evoke sexual anxiety states in the listeners' own bodies. *Political* speeches are verifiable against the people's own bodily processes.' (Theweleit, 1989, 107)

In fact, Theweleit is issuing a critique of the left and of its failure to comprehend the call to bodily response that permeates popular politics. He berates the left (and German sociology) for relying on dry argument and the addition of information, when the 'primary territory of effectivity is elsewhere' (109). The elsewhere in question is the unspoken but ever-present recesses of the body, and the appeal of authoritarian leaders is based on a promise to the populace 'to guide them for they fear they will lose themselves on, across, within their own bodies or in the far greater mysteries of other bodies – the body of the people' (Theweleit, 1989, 108). The dynamic of such bodily appeals also illuminates the role of non-information and declared secrecy in governmental processes in eliciting grateful acquiescence from the public, a set of practices with clear echoes in our time:

> announcement of long-term news blackouts becomes a source of pleasure for millions (in a situation in which the information content of the news is in any case negligible). Ringed with the aura of high security, politics at last becomes interesting: we are being told nothing, *ergo* we are being governed. Oh joy! (Theweleit, 1989, 109)

The War on Terror does not demand such active joy from those subject to authoritarian governance. However, the recognition that an element of declared secrecy can signal the reassuring power of the state has been incorporated into War on Terror strategies of governance. The sense that we are being told just enough keeps us fearful of hearing more.

Embodying dangerous men

There is an extensive literature analysing the central role of visual representations in creating mythologies of racialised masculinity (hooks, 1992; Carby, 2000). This hypervisibility has been explained as an indication of social degradation. Whereas powerful groups have sought to gather the symbolic status of the phallus to themselves, as if mystifying and erasing the leaky humanity of some bodies would allow that unspeakable phallic law to accrue to weak, fleshy but resolutely invisible penises, the insistent exposure of some other men indicates their lack of social status.

In his survey of surveillance in America, Christian Parenti argues both that systems of identification and surveillance have developed as techniques of institutionalised racist oppression and that modern criminal justice systems are formulated around such systems of identification and surveillance. These two themes have not always been in easy alignment. For example, Parenti describes the rising use of photography as a policing technique in the urban centres of nineteenth-century America and Europe and the limitations of this apparent recording of a 'truthful' image:

> photography was a powerful tool only if a suspect could be matched to an image, a task that was easier said than done. And the more photos police produced, the harder became the process of sorting, organizing, and using them. With hundreds, even thousands of images on file, how were the photos to be archived? By name, physical description, numerical code? (Parenti, 2003, 39)

At the same time as this burgeoning data collection was occurring in the cities of America and Europe, such proliferating records of surveillance were regarded as inadequate for the purposes of colonial administration. Colonised populations were regarded as unsuitable for facial record-keeping. Instead, techniques such as dactylography, fingerprinting, gained ground as a method that overcame the apparent homogeneity of darker-skinned bodies and faces:

> white administrators and police who saw (or imagined) Asians, Africans, and native Americans as bafflingly homogeneous began to fall back on the infinite uniqueness of fingerprints. Thus, fingerprinting literally migrated from colonial periphery to the economic core. In the United States the first populations to be fingerprinted en masse were convicts, petty criminals, soldiers, and Native peoples. (Parenti, 2003, 49)

As Parenti and others have written, affluent nations are experiencing an escalation in levels of surveillance in everyday life, a collation of information for the overlapping purposes of commerce, governance, policing and national security. However there is a discrepancy between the promise of greater knowledge and security from increased surveillance and the depiction of terrorist extremism as demonic precisely because so invisibly hidden in our midst. Although nations such as the US, Britain and Australia appear to champion the benefits of ethnic profiling as an effective method of identifying terrorist threats, this trust in the visible markings of difference is contradicted by the parallel narratives of secret cells, home-grown terrorists and shadowy migrants who cross borders without leaving a trace.

In an echo of previous eras of heightened surveillance, the War on Terror mobilises the two contradictory beliefs that everything and everyone must be watched and monitored but that the unimaginable evil that motivates terrorism is invisible to the uninitiated. In this context, the insistent referencing of the physical embodiment of free and unfree femininity and barbaric and civilised masculinity serves as a guide to identifying the boundaries between us and them, but also as a reminder of the malleability and unreadability of human bodies. On the one hand there is a reaffirmation of racialised boundaries of differ-ence, a set of differences based not only on physical characteristics but also on the more nuanced reading of how the body is staged, as seen in the renewed use of ethnic profiling for a range of security purposes. On the other there is the repeated suggestion that terrorism is such a threat because so invisible, hidden beneath a veneer of apparent normality, fired by unfathomable conversions to fanaticism, as discussed in the wide-ranging speculation about the motives and formation of those suspected of the 7/7 bombings. In this second theme, physical markers act as a misleading decoy. The evil terrorist has learned to manipulate western culture and to mimic its bodily staging. It is westernisation that is seen to characterise the terrorist mastermind.

3

State Racism and Muslim Men as a Racialised Threat

The dynamics of racism within developed nations have always been shaped by the global politics of 'race', both the histories of slavery and empire and the ongoing divisions of the world along racialised lines of exploitation (Winant, 2001). However, the urgency of local issues has sometimes occluded these global connections. Now, in this time of so-called 'new imperialism' (Harvey, 2003; Mooers, 2006), it is no longer tenable to pretend that the immediate interests of racialised communities in different locations are distinct from the larger battles against imperialism and flesh-eating capital. The so-called War on Terror, recently renamed 'the long war', has seeped into the politics of 'race' in America, Britain and beyond. Racialised policing continues, now with the additional intensity of 'combating terrorism'. Familiar racist mythologies are revamped to fit new fears about dangerous extremists in our midst. Minority communities are challenged to prove their allegiance and integration, however long they have been settled in the 'host' nation. Everyday racism takes up the rhetoric of recent wars and transforms minorities once again into 'enemies within' who must be tamed and contained by a highly militarised state racism (Kundnani, 2007).

This book has argued that the War on Terror combines overt and covert military engagement with a wider cultural project that, among other things, attempts to rework the internal contracts of citizenship in the nations of the 'coalition of the willing' and perhaps beyond. There is no suggestion that this is a conspiracy to augment state power and repress dissent. However I do want to argue that gaining popular consent for greater levels of unchecked state intervention in everyday life, including greater levels of state-sanctioned violence, is an important component in the construction of models of national security and public culture. This chapter analyses the processes by which the contract between state and citizen have subtly altered and argues that an Islamicisation of older racial categories has served to justify such state tactics. This is a process that at once builds on techniques of state racism and circulates a developed critique and disavowal of racism. In its place, a combination of cultural and ideological difference is posited as the danger requiring the rational and justifiable response of state racism.

The War on Terror and state racisms

Debates about state racism have returned in recent years. After a period where great energies were devoted to exploring cultural formations and identity constructions, discussion has turned again to the state machineries that administer racial categorisation and the characteristics that tip such activity into racism (Goldberg, 2002). For our purposes it is not necessary to prove that the liberal state is, in fact, a racist state, although this is the argument proposed by a variety of activists and other commentators (Lentin and Lentin, 2006).

My interest is in the working of state racism in this time and in relation to both the cultural constructions and the emerging transnational security machinery of the War on Terror. I want to argue that the War on Terror is a project that seeks to rewrite the terms of international relations and at the same time to relegitimise state racism within particular locations. This chapter will consider the playing out of this relegitimised state racism in a number of contexts and argue that this represents a militarisation of everyday life.

There are two key elements of this trend. One is the resurrection of a plethora of racist mythologies that mobilise ideas of threat, invasion and competition in order to encourage repression and marginalisation of targeted minorities (Fekete, 2001). The other is the development of policing and other state practices that are informed by the techniques of security services and which are shaped by the pressure to co-operate across borders in the pursuit of a shared and militarised security agenda (King, 2006; Loader, 2002).

As an example, in Britain this has taken the form of a combination of old-fashioned racist policing, now reinforced by the widely accepted concept of ethnic profiling (Goodey, 2006; Hallsworth, 2006), and a series of legal developments that indicate an explicit shift away from such troublesome anachronisms as the assumption of innocence or the right to a fair trial. Similar initiatives have been taken in a variety of other national spaces, as will be discussed below. For now, it is enough to note that the War on Terror heralds a shift in the internal policing and security practices of individual nations and that such shifts have tended to combine the continuing demonisation of local target groups with significant extensions of state powers.

Not the first time

Before we continue too far down this route, it is important to remember that much of this is all too familiar to anyone who has had an interest in the conduct of policing. The large and respected body of literature that documents and analyses the manner and intent of racist policing reminds us that this is no aberration (for some examples see Bowling, 1998; Rowe, 2004). This is not some sudden failure of liberal institutions in the face of the horror of terrorism. Rather these abuses at the edge of the system have characterised the institution of policing since its inception (Waddington, 1999). Now as always the contract of everyday lawfulness relies on the liminal creature who cannot abide by such agreements. This is the body that allows the law to enact its powers and to demonstrate both the danger of disobedience and the benefits of protection.

There is nothing new about policing that is influenced by militarised tactics. The experience of Northern Ireland revealed how easily policing and military occupation could slide into each other (Ellison and Smyth, 2000). Tactics from Ireland were used against targeted groups in Britain – trade unionists became the enemy within and the 1984–5 miners' strike witnessed the advent of highly militarised and intimidatory policing tactics against pickets (Richards, 1997).

If we consider these earlier instances, it becomes clear that elements of militarised policing have existed alongside the famed consensual policing of liberal societies for some time. The policing tactics used in relation to liminal spaces such as picket lines, poor and minority neighbourhoods and, most of all, contested colonies demonstrate the tactics that are used against groups who are viewed not as full citizens but as enemy aliens who threaten the nation.

I am identifying a range of factors as indicative of militarisation, whether through a refusal of civilian codes of conduct in relation to levels of force or civilian–officer interaction or through a curtailment of the due process of law. Some of the key characteristics of this process are outlined here:

- *The greater level of force.* The claim that this is a war situation enables militarised policing to use greater levels of force against civilians, including through the use of equipment that would be banned or restricted in other circumstances.
- *The erosion of due process.* There is a lesser adherence to proper process and a lesser attention to the rights of suspects, again justified by the rhetoric of emergency and the demonisation of the out-group as a threat to the greater good.
- *Changes in the presentation and accessibility of officers.* Uniform becomes a de-civilianising accessory, involving the disruption of proper accountability between officers and civilians by the hiding of identifying marks such as numbers, while there is also a blurring of the boundary between protective clothing and clothing intended to intimidate: the use of masks and shields for example.
- *Occupation policing.* Saturation deployment of police in certain areas in order to subdue the local population through a demon-stration of intimidatory force.

Each of these elements serves to increase the scope and discretion of state authority, adding to the overall process of militarisation as a shift in the relation between citizen and state. Popular consent is maintained both through the intensive deployment of demonising propaganda and through the implication that such regrettable but necessary abuses do not occur in ordinary civilian spaces but instead are a part of the Wild West uncertainties of spaces of exclusion. Importantly, this conception of the space of lawlessness operates alongside the continuing functioning of consensus-policing for some.

More recently, the identification of certain areas as beyond the rule of ordinary law has enabled the machinery of everyday militarisation to be refined and extended. I will go on to consider how such developments build on other initiatives that have sought to create outsider groups through the practices of policing.

The conduct of the War on Terror rewrites the terms of state–citizen relations and the application of law, but this rewriting occurs in a manner that allows a continuation of polite policing for many (for accounts of this process see, Peschek, 2005; Kellner, 2003). When lawyers and civil liberties campaigners complain of the emergence of a police state, they forget that such claims appear nonsensical to much of the population. The rule of law has not been dismantled. Policing and law and order continue to function in familiar ways for most people. The erosions of legal rights are experienced primarily by groups deemed outside the contract of societal belonging; and this loss of rights is associated with whatever deficiency defines this state of unbelonging. One way or another, the majority population are encouraged to believe that erosions of the rule of law are not a threat to them. Rather these retreats from recognised legal process are a necessary evil if the majority is to be protected.

This framework of different laws and legal status for different groups of people echoes the classic characteristics of the racial state. Both the establishment of a category of less-than-citizen who does not enjoy the legal rights of the rest of the population and the cultural assault that asserts that it is necessary for the good of the majority that the minority should suffer are reminiscent of the practices of racial and racist states (Goldberg, 2002). Here the difference is not specified as a racial category and the plethora of anti-terrorist legislation and initiatives that have sprung up around the world cannot be characterised as race laws in any straightforward way. However, the War on Terror has given rise to state practices that are, at least, reminiscent of the governance techniques of racial states.

Establishing the category of the less-than-human

In Britain, this process builds on the campaigns conducted against migrants and the idea of migration through successive Asylum and Immigration Acts. These legislative developments took place as one aspect of a far larger project to shape public attitudes to migration and the role of the state. Admittedly, such strategies are themselves an outcome of a longstanding antipathy to migrants within the popular and political culture of the country (see Knox, 1999; Money, 1999). State responses have been an attempt to capitalise on this popular sentiment. Until recently, there was little sense that government viewed migrants as a problem that impinged on other governmental goals, although this has become a central aspect of more recent anti-migrant declarations. Previously, political mobilisation of anti-migrant feeling appeared to be motivated almost entirely by a desire to capture the anti-migrant feeling in the country in order to reap the political benefits of that association (Saggar, 2003). However at the same time, the framing and public discussion of legislative change also becomes part of this creation of specific migrant monsters. This is one important theme that is shared by anti-immigration and anti-terrorism laws. In both cases, the public presentation and debating of proposed legislation itself become part of the cultural battle around the issue. Arguably, the introduction of such proposals in itself has served as a significant component of the demonisation of the target groups.

Anti-migrant state activity in the UK not only conjures up a popular response that legitimises repressive state measures, but also both creates new offences that criminalise migrants both in the public imagination and in law and extends the powers of the state in a manner that erodes standards of decency and fairness.

Analysts of the politics of migration suggest that a similar dynamic has applied in other locations (Fetzer, 2000). Michael Welch analyses the long-running scapegoating and pathologisation of immigrants in the United States and examines the processes that have led to an increasing criminalisation of migrants. Welch identifies what he terms 'court-stripping provisions' that emerged from 1996 changes in immigration law and from legislation to curtail the rights of prisoners and the simultaneous institution of the use of secret evidence (Welch, 2002, 66–72). Such developments collapse immigration, terrorism and criminality into one multi-headed demon, a monster that demands that the protections of law and a fair hearing are curtailed for the greater good.

US scholarship analysing the emergence of a 'new penology' has identified the continuum between prisoner abuse within national borders and the treatment of detainees in the global War on Terror (Dow, 2005; Parenti, 2000; Davis, 1999). Welch outlines the violence, degradation and sexual abuse suffered by immigration detainees in the US, citing reports of mob beatings carried out by guards (104, 121–3), sexual assault and rape (123–5), and rituals demonstrating the absolute power of prison guards over prisoners and detainees such as forcing men to kneel while naked and chant 'America is No.1' (104). Welch and others place these events in the context of a massively expanded penal system that disproportionately imprisons African-American and Hispanic-American people, and that is shaped by a virulently racist popular panic and the emergence of a prison-industrial complex that turns prisons into methods of hyper-exploitation and profit creation.

The extensive reports of abuse of immigrants in the various systems of immigration control, detention and removal indicates the extent to which anti-migrant law and state activity have served to divide the population into those deserving of legal rights and corresponding treatment and those who fall outside this contract. More than this, the incremental increase in dehumanising treatment for migrants at the hands of the law has created a climate in which many have come to accept that some groups of people can be treated in this manner. In Britain this can be seen in popular acquiescence to deportations of asylum-seekers to war-ravaged Iraq or of the terminally ill to an accelerated death without adequate health care. An additional outcome of popular anti-migrant sentiment has been the acceptance that the law need not apply to all people and a view among some that it is better if it does not.

Key elements of anti-migrant campaigns anticipate actions taken in the name of the War on Terror. Detention without trial, in particular, has become institutionalised in Britain and America as a method of deterring would-be migrants. In the process, an alternative penal system has emerged as a precursor to the well-known excesses of the War on Terror. Mark Dow, for example, argues that details of post-September 11 detention policies were not surprising to immigrant advocates, because they were familiar with these patterns of violence, abuse and mistaken identity from their work with immigration detainees (Dow, 2005, 13). Dow argues that the exercise of US immigration control is punctuated by an unchecked racism on the part of immigration officers (69). Alternatively, the excessive power allocated to immigration officers can turn an immigration application into an occasion to enact a crude homophobia:

> She [immigration officer and witness] also recalls asylum applicants who claimed fear of persecution based on their sexual orientation. INS officers would force those applicants to show their 'walk' in order to 'prove' they were gay. (Dow, 2005, 69)

In this example, the abuse is explicitly homophobic and directed at those who have self-identified as lesbian, gay or bisexual. However, the manner of the enforced and humiliating performance is reminiscent of accounts of detainee abuse in other contexts. Dow also recounts an incident suffered by a US immigration detainee, Oviawe, that seems to anticipate the ritualistic abuses of Abu Ghraib. After a series of harsh beatings during the detainees' transfer to another prison, a further stage of abuse followed:

> 'So we were now taken to the cell. "Get into the cell." We were asked to strip ourself naked. Three of us: myself, a Ghanian, and another Indian boy. We were three. We were asked to strip ourself naked, right in the cell there. Then we were asked to kneel down. We were asked to be on our knee. You are naked. Then, the next person to you, you grab his ear, you draw him by the ear, as you are on your knee, then the other one would drag the other person. We were there for more than three hours.' In the Canarsie living room, Oviawe explains that he and his two cellmates formed a small circle, each holding the ears of the person in front of him. 'The guards, they started coming around. When they come around, one of them, very huge guy, he spat mucus. In short, it was so horrible. You understand? Some other [officers] started coming, to come and see if we had ever stood up from that kneel. We were there for more than three hours.' (Dow, 2005, 142)

Dow collates the testimony of many immigration prisoners and their experience anticipates central aspects of War on Terror detention in a number of ways. They are subject to random violence, often at the whim of racist officials; they are forced to act out painful and sexually humiliating scenarios, apparently for the amusement of their guards; their holy books are desecrated and thrown into toilets; they are subject to an imprisonment that may have no end and where the length of detention bears no relation to the alleged infringement. Each of these can be recognised as a precursor to the treatment of terrorist suspects in the War on Terror. However, my point is not only to identify the continuity of abusive techniques between immigration and War on Terror detention. Of equal significance is the establishment of a widely accepted precedent for excluding some groups from the legal rights and entitlements of the majority population. The intensive campaigning and activity against migrants across a range of developed and less developed nations has served this purpose very effectively.

If there is any doubt about the impact of anti-migrant state activity on wider concepts of legality and acceptability, a brief consideration of the treatment of refugee children reveals the extent to which the treatment of migrants has instituted a parallel space of emergency beyond the law. Lisa Nandy reminds us that international agreements such as the United Nations Convention on the Rights of the Child demand that 'the best interests of the child should be a primary consideration in all decisions affecting them' (Nandy, 2005, 411). Despite this, Britain specifies that these rights do not apply to children who are subject to immigration control, leading to a situation where refugee children are detained 'solely for administrative purposes' (Nandy, 2005, 411). Not only are many migrants detained without charge for indefinite periods, this group includes significant numbers of children, and this practice is widespread across Europe. Liz Fekete explains that these detentions violate international law:

> International law places the needs of children (defined as those under the age of 18) above the requirements of immigration control. When used other than as a measure of 'last resort', the detention of children for the purposes of immigration control violates international standards for the treatment of children set out by the UN Convention on the Rights of the Child (UNCRC), the UNHCR and the UN Rules on Juveniles Deprived of their Liberty (UN JDL Rules). It even goes against the grain of a recent EU Council Directive which states that 'the best interests of the child shall be a primary consideration' when dealing with minors seeking asylum. (Fekete, 2007, 94)

Yet despite this a range of European nations, including Norway, Denmark, Britain, Switzerland, France, Greece, Spain, Italy and Belgium, all detain child refugees, often in adult prisons and with little regard for the well-being and safety of the child. This willingness to imprison large numbers of children as a deterrent to would-be migrants indicates the extent to which European publics have come to accept that some groups do not and should not enjoy the protection of the law and due process. Once this duality has been established for that most vulnerable group, children, it is a small step to accept that other groups also may fall outside the realm of legal rights.

Why 'militarisation'?

A key aspect of what I am describing as militarisation is the process by which segments of national space are excluded from the reach of domestic law and the expectations of due process. This process is justified as a necessary response to a war situation, and the alternative legal framework that is imposed is presented as a domesticated version of the law of war.

Elements of such exclusions were evident in a range of locations before the War on Terror. Curbs on the right to protest or to gather for outdoor parties had already been framed in a such a manner as to create zones of emergency where police powers would be enhanced and the rights of citizens would be curtailed (McKay, 1998). The claim that states may have recourse to emergency measures in situations of threat to the nation is recognised and regulated in human rights treaties (Yotopoulos and Benedek, 2004). However, initiatives against public protests or outdoor gatherings instituted a concept of emergency while falling short of suggesting a general state of emergency. This resulted in a granting of greater authority and discretion to police, but within seemingly controlled conditions.

The division of national space into zones of emergency and zones of civilian law calls on old tropes in the history of policing (for an account of the contested workings of such distinctions, see Johnson, 2003). Consent to the authority of the police force requires a recognition of the legitimacy of that force and an acceptance that some other is deserving of police intervention. Part of this acceptance of the role of the police has been a belief in the safeguard of due process and a fair trial. These are the things that make police power more than brute force against the vulnerable. Curtailing the right to a fair trial and otherwise pulling back the expectations of due process of law renders ordinary citizens completely vulnerable to the arbitrary discretion of police powers. For such an attack on the rights of the civilian population to be acceptable, there needs to be some assurance that only some kinds of people, those deserving of such curtailments of rights, will come under these powers. Through a variety of narratives, zones of emergency are presented as methods of containing the dangerous periphery of those at the edge of societal belonging, whether they are the roughs, the undeserving poor (Websdale, 2001), the dross (Choongh, 1997), the enemy within (Green, 1992), black muggers (Hall et al., 1978) or Muslim fundamentalists.

In Britain the creeping erosion of the rule of law has been narrated increasingly as a necessary cost for the maintenance of national security. Those who fall under the auspices of the emergency powers granted to police under public order and anti-terrorism laws are, by definition, threats to the nation.

Unlike explicitly racist states, such laws do not specify that some groups will be subject to this law while others – the majority, the privileged who enjoy state sanction – are not. There is an attempt to retain the link between action and state intervention, but in this case it is movement into the specified zone that makes you into a dangerous alien. In practice it is almost impossible to be sure if you are in civilian or emergency space and such zones are in a constant state of flux. In particular, recent UK legislation in relation to both anti-social behaviour and anti-terrorism enables police to exercise a great deal of discretion in the application of emergency powers. However, the fiction continues that this formulation allows normal life to continue unhampered for the innocent while enabling suitable and discretionary security measures only against those who make themselves vulnerable by straying into emergency space. Similarly, the Bush administration has favoured a military justice approach, but has not been consistent in its application:

> Thus, John Walker Lindh, the 'American Taliban,' was permitted to plead guilty to criminal charges in a United States District Court in Alexandria, Virginia. The factual parallels between Lindh's case and that of Yaser Esam Hamdi are striking. Yet Hamdi remains in detention, held without criminal charges at the Naval Brig in Norfolk, Virginia. The exceptions exemplified by the Lindh case and by the recent criminal conviction of the 'Al-Qaeda shoe-bomber' Richard Reid do not necessarily indicate that the administration has departed from its apparent preference for the military justice model.' (Stephens, 2004, 60)

Militarisation is not, therefore, only or primarily an issue of levels of force, although the unleashing of greater police discretion has tended to lead to more state violence against vulnerable groups. The militarisation of everyday life is also a process that erodes the right of citizens to civil solutions by proclaiming the pressing needs of national security. In this, this is an everyday militarisation that combines actual shifts in state practice and a wider, more diffuse cultural project that presents these shifts as necessary and contained losses in the face of a greater enemy.

There are some obvious components of this erosion of civilian space. For example, the widespread acceptance of greater levels of personal search at airports and other nodal points and the vilification of civil liberties campaigners who suggest that such initiatives may be unnecessary and counterproductive is a small indication of the manner in which individuals appear to be accepting the right of the state to treat all as suspects (see, for example, 'Human Rights is Merely a Sweetner for Rapists, Murderers and Violent Criiminals, Allison Pearson, *Daily Mail*, 6/11/07). There may be (many) cases of minor cheating and ridicule but such games confirm that the overall process has been accepted and internalised, with resistance reduced to childish japes (Allison, 2004).

This matters less than the wider acceptance of state authority as a legitimate purveyor of violence in everyday life. There may be a muttered dissatisfaction with detention without trial, with greater stop-and-search, and with the intrusion of surveillance and scrutiny into all arenas of life, but, on the whole, all such measures are accepted grudgingly as necessary if Big Brother tells us so. The War on Terror represents, in those nations where these terms have currency, the opportunity to suggest a state of emergency without actually instituting such a labour-intensive and costly measure. The cultural project of suggesting emergency, as opposed to the actual intensive activity required to institute such a state officially (Chowdhury, 1989), seeks to transform the civilian population into a body more amenable and accepting and less questioning of state authority. What shifts is the relation between state and citizen, with far greater emphasis on the grateful duties required for the gift of citizenship, most of all for those lucky enough to live in the liberal freedom of western democracy. This combined with the continuance of a long history of racist belief and expectation enables the institution of a racist state in effect, while maintaining a disavowal of racism in official discourse.

Sexualised racism and religious unreason

Some attention has been given in recent scholarship to new racial myths from our new and differently racialised times (Institute of Race Relations, 2001). In fact, these supposedly new myths build extensively on much older histories of sex, race and unreason, and earlier scholarship examining these issues can appear disconcertingly contemporary on rereading. For example, Sander Gilman has written extensively about the linkages between European conceptions of race, sexual depravity and mental illness. In this work, he has returned continually to the issue of the physicalisation of Jewish identity. He explains his project thus, in a defence against the allegation that all this talk of representation is merely a concern with labelling: 'I am engrossed by the ideological implications associated with the image of the Jews (and other groups) as "different"' (Gilman, 1991, 2).

A number of important issues are contained in this statement. First, there is the reiteration of the importance of cultural analysis in order to comprehend the worldly impact of such cultural traces. Second, there is the description of being fixed as a spectator before the staging of difference. Third, there is the assertion that the ideological work is carried out through depicting Jews and others as 'different'. I am interested in this suggestion that the representation of difference as pathological seeks to transfix the audience in an attitude of spectatorship. Such a suggestion clearly chimes with the discussion of earlier chapters and the sense that demeaning representations of certain groups can serve to discipline members of the group in part through positioning them as complicit in their viewing of these images.

For now, the key insight from Gilman is his discussion of how the Jewish male is embodied in racist discourse and the repeated assertion that expressions of anti-Semitism, whether fixated on religious justifications, cultural differences, political threats or expedient scape-goating, all reference Jewishness as an identity tied to the body: 'the central figure throughout is that of the male Jew, the body with the circumcised penis – an image crucial to the very understanding of the Western image of the Jew at least since the advent of Christianity' (Gilman, 1991, 5). Although Gilman has written famously and influentially on the representation of race, gender and sexuality in the nineteenth century and the depiction of black women through this framework, he is adamant that the image at the heart of anti-Semitic discourse is that of a man, a man who is defined by the lack of a foreskin: 'it is *this* representation which I believe lies at the very heart of Western Jew-hatred' (Gilman, 1991, 5).

It is significant that Gilman places the image of the Jewish male's body at the centre of this narrative. The account given is of bodily scrutiny, an endless objectification and fantasy of what the Jew's body means. To focus so intensively on the male body in this process, with little parallel energy given to imagining the nature and meaning of the Jewish female body, must indicate something about the manner of this racist characterisation. After all, there has been no lack of objectification and scrutiny of the female body. In fact, Gilman himself identifies key processes of pathologisation, sexualisation and objectification of women's bodies in his analysis of ideas of degeneracy. However, in these discussions the pathology of Jewishness remains focused on the male body. Jewish pathology may be seen to parallel the degeneracy of other supposedly deviant groups such as Africans and prostitutes, but the embodiment of this pathology remains insistently male.

I am interested in this account of a racist mythology that is so fascinated with the bodies of the (men of the) despised group, not least because there appear to be some obvious parallels with present-day racisms.

The anti-Muslim racism of recent times is less open in its objectification and scrutiny of the male Muslim body. The techniques used to physicalise difference in nineteenth-century Europe brought together anxieties about gender and sexuality, emerging popular imagination about race, madness and disease, and the role of science in identifying social-cum-physiological dangers or anomalies. Contemporary science and culture are less overtly focused on the physicalisation of difference. However, there is something in the various and intensive focus on the dangers of Muslim men that echoes those earlier constructions of Jew-hating.

Gilman's focus on the male incarnation of the hated identity and his insistence that it is Jewish *masculinity* that is the focus of anti-Semitic scrutiny and hatred is instructive for our times. Alongside this, the account of the transformation of religious culture into a marker of wider degeneracy – and the implication that such degeneracy can be read through the body – also echoes the accelerating demonisation of Muslims in recent times.

For Gilman, the articulation of anti-Semitism returns again and again to an anxiety about male circumcision. This is the marker of the dangerous Jewish man, the identifier of a suspect community who claim the right to adjust nature as their cultural duty, and who personify the ability to change shape and hide inner degeneracy through physical modification.

There are a number of implications in such an account. First, the suggestion that the dominant group projects sexual anxieties, not least the fear of castration, onto others who come to be embodied by their practices of bodily modification. From this, there is an implication that circumcised communities themselves come to embody the terror of castration – and, perhaps even more fearfully, represent the possibility of survival in this mutilated form.

In accounts of other sexualised racisms, most famously in relation to racist fantasies of the black man and his mythical penis, the scrutiny of the body of the subordinated man is an indication of the insecurities of the powerful. This is racism as a battle between men, played out through the demonstration of masculine prowess and comparison of masculine attributes (Clegg, 1994). The fixation on the Jewish male body has had elements of this sexualised competition as shown in a host of anti-Semitic stereotypes from wily seducer to white-slave-trader to spreader/carrier of syphilis to alien rapist. Although these mythologies have existed in parallel with ideas of a feminised Jewish male who is too degenerate or too cerebral to be a real man, there is also this strand of sexual fascination in racist mythologies of Jewishness (Felsenstein, 1995; Cheyette, 1996).

Susan Bordo focuses on the myth of feminised Jewish man when she highlights the representation in Nazi literature of Jewish masculinity as 'dwarfish, womanish, simpering, impotent' (Bordo, 1999, 49) and suggests that these images are linked to the fixation on the 'foreshortened' penis. Bordo goes on to revisit Freud's account of nursery rumours of circumcision and the explanation that Jews are hated because Jewish men seem to embody the threat of castration.

However other accounts of histories of circumcision seem to contradict this, admittedly well-known, account. More recent studies of the practice of male circumcision have suggested that this modification may impair the sexual pleasure of the adult male, and that circumcision comes to be regarded as a social good only in a framework of normative heterosexual intercourse that limits the conception of sexuality to the reproductive act (Richters, 2006). Linked to this is the suggestion that circumcision is a process that seeks to solidify and make visible the male–female dyad by refashioning the penis into a closer approximation of phallicity. In this telling, circumcision is another practice designed to render the alleged natural binary of gender tangible. Interestingly, such an attempt is linked to other practices that heighten the visibility and significance of secondary sexual characteristics such as the growing of beards (Richters, 2006).

In earlier periods, circumcision was recommended for supposedly medical reasons in part as a corrective against masturbation (Darby, 2003). The circumcised man raises the double spectre of the containment of desire and the release of such desire by other means – both too disciplined and too anarchic, in the manner of the demasculinised Jew and the revolutionary terrorist. The combined strands of racist fear that have been attributed to male religious circumcision could be seen as anticipating the sexualised account of Muslim radicalisation, a disorder that is presented as stemming from Muslim men being at once too insistently and inflexibly masculine and yet, at the same time, in the sexual arena not man enough. These competing myths, after all, have animated anti-Semitic rumour for centuries.

In an essay considering the double markers of Jewish masculinity, circumcision and head covering, Jonathan Boyarin reviews some representations of the place of circumcision in marking boundaries. 'Consideration for a moment of the fact that for a long time Europe's Others consisted of Jews, Turks, "Saracens", and "Moors" – all circumcised, of course – yields the surprising implication that uncircumcision becomes ultimately the diacritic of Christianness' (Boyarin, 1996, 41)

The bodily modification of circumcision thus serves as an indicator of belonging and unbelonging in both directions and as the factor underlying construction of mythologies of sexual depravity and sexual dysfunction (Darby, 2003) – both of which are portrayed as at the root of social danger.

It is tempting to argue for a parallel between these largely European racisms and the demonisation of Muslims that is scurrying across and between national borders in our time. It appears to be so helpful a connection. Muslim men have come to occupy a similar space to that of Jewish men in the racist imaginary, embodying at once a dangerous hypermasculinity and a mutilated deviation from proper manhood. They too are portrayed as impenetrable, secretive, enmeshed in an alien culture that inhabits the secret places of an unsuspecting host society. Their masculinity is regarded as excessive and dysfunctional, too absolute in the internalisation of restraint, too refusing of desire or of malleability, too literal in their understanding of ideal masculinity. Circumcision could represent the link between these two racialised myths, an indication of how cultures of bodily modification can come to embody the racist fears of others. It all fits so well.

However, whatever Gilman and others may write about the centrality of circumcision to racist depictions of Jewish men, contemporary representations of masculinity tend to be less obviously medicalised and, perhaps more importantly, circumcision does not at present mark the boundary between Christendom and its others. Circumcision remains the norm in the United States, across cultural communities. Other multi-ethnic and multi-religious societies retain significant minorities of circumcised men. This is no longer the marker between 'us' and 'them' that Boyarin describes.

Bodies and beliefs

Although contemporary demonisation of Muslims includes a particular mythology of the body, it is hard to discern the place of a fantastical circumcised penis in this myth. Instead, the religious racism of our time portrays sexual dysfunction and gender excess as an outcome of religious excess. Too much fervour in the arena of faith distorts and diverts energy from the proper pursuit of sexuality, a pursuit that has become an important marker of normality and individualisation in our time (for a highly controversial presentation of these ideas see Amis, 2006; for a critique see Abu Khalil, 2001).

The War on Terror contains an ambivalence about the proper place of religion. On the one hand, proponents are keen to appeal to their faith, their morality and even their god(s) when presenting the case for continuing war (Greene, 2003; Blond and Pabst, 2006; Stam, 2003; Baker, 2006; Beattie, 2007). On the other, international terrorism is regarded as an outcome of distorted and excessive belief (Esposito, 2002). This is where religion can go and, in part, the War on Terror is an attempt to contain this possibility.

However this is not an easy divide between religious and secular viewpoints, although some would wish to portray it as such. Left and liberal supporters of the invasions of Afghanistan and Iraq have presented themselves as defenders of Enlightenment values of reason and progress, against the backward barbarism of stultifying religion (Cohen, 2007). However the public pronouncements of Bush, Blair and their allies have not proclaimed their proud adherence to the values of secularism. Although debates about multiculturalism and its backlash have reinvigorated self-identified secularists, those closer to the apparatus of global power have presented themselves as humble believers (for a discussion of secularism in international relations, see Hurd, 2004).

The plethora of discussion has nudged towards the suggestion that it is Islam, and Islam alone, that represents a dangerous extremism of belief. This suggestion lingers despite the many assertions that extremists do not represent the majority of Muslims and that Islam is not in its essence an extremist tradition (Ramadan, 2004). This is a racialisation that builds on the insights of anti-racist critiques and the lessons of postcolonial theory. Thus this monstrous Islam is historically specific, not timeless; forged in the messy and dishonest negotiations of the dying Cold War; with a particular material base and an explicably articulated doctrine; shaped by the inequalities and perceived injustices of globalisation – altogether a demon of our times, brought to life through the careful analysis of a new orientalism that knows to avoid the pitfalls of generalisation, anachronism and mythologisation.

And yet, despite all of this care and contextual information, the enemy remains an absolute and essentialised figure of Islam.

Binyam Mohamed has described his horrific experiences of being extraordinarily rendered and tortured in a number of locations before being transferred to Guantánamo. Part of the frighteningly imaginative torture that he suffered for many days was a strange and truly terrifying ritual in which his penis was cut many times with a sharp scalpel. When they made cuts all over his body and poured salt solution into the cuts they also cut his private parts saying it would be better to just cut his penis off as he would only breed more terrorists (Stafford Smith, 2007).

I began this work in response to the case of Binyam Mohamed, and, because I know his name and cannot name the thousands of others detained in the secret and illegal prisons of the War on Terror, I think of his case as emblematic of the horror and character of War on Terror torture. The terrible creativity of the violence, the fixation on genitalia – these are characteristics that can be seen in other scenes of sexualised racial violence and I have some knowledge of both how such theatricalised abuse operates and how it can be understood as a component of a larger culture of oppression and violence (Bhattacharyya, 1998; Bhattacharyya, Gabriel and Small, 2001). I have tried to argue throughout this work that the sexualisation of racism and violence is not incidental, but instead is a significant component of the workings of the War on Terror. Other incidents confirm this view. Khaled El Masri, a German citizen, was abducted by the CIA and also subjected to highly sexualised torture, including penetration of his rectum using a blunt instrument. Reports from Guantánamo repeatedly point to the use of sexualised assault and sexual humiliation as supposed interrogation methods (Otterman, 2007). Abu Ghraib staged the War on Terror through the lens of sadistic pornography. The horrific use of sexual torture and violence appears to employ a version of cultural knowledge in order to heighten the humiliation (Strasser, 2004).

Well-known accounts of US interrogation techniques confirm this sense that the techniques of intercultural understanding have come to inform this other world (McCoy, 2006). Despite the apparent knowingness of statements that proclaim the benefits of western tolerance for diverse societies, the deployment of this supposed cultural knowledge in the processes of torture reveals an image of an essentialised Muslim man, a man who truly can be broken only through the cultural pressure point of sexual humiliation. This racist myth enables the dual suggestions that all other violence, however extreme, has no impact and that the barbarism of these people is demonstrated by their backward beliefs about sex.

The War on Terror and everyday life in the West

This book seeks to show how the War on Terror functions as a cultural project to transform social relations and expectations across nations. This is not to ignore the significance of the recognisable battle sites of this war or of the continuing destruction and loss of life. However, as key proponents have asserted repeatedly, this project extends far beyond Afghanistan and Iraq and other identifiable theatres of war. The reach of the War on Terror includes such disparate aspects as domestic order debates, child-rearing practices, the reach of police powers, the exercise of the law and, only alongside all these things, explicit military intervention. In the process it scoops up a range of localised power struggles that span Asia and Latin America as well as the Middle East, Europe and the US.

Additionally, the War on Terror represents an attempt to reshape public perceptions of threat, the role of the state, and the proper exercise of law. In practice this reshaping can take place only through the diffuse cultural means of contestation through public discourse. Military might and economic leverage may ensure that you can control some outcomes in the world, but how people think and feel is not yet one of them.

In fact, part of what is distinctive about the War on Terror is the intermeshing of representational strategies and a practical machinery of containment. Participation in the 'coalition of the willing' has not only entailed support for US-led military interventions but also has been demonstrated through the creation of new legislation to meet the terrorist threat. Such developments are a tangible method of showing that we are in a new era. Existing law is presented as inadequate to the task of prosecuting crimes of international terrorism, even though international terrorism is not a new phenomenon and the acts contained under this heading could be designated as other, more familiar types of offence.

The creation of new legislation serves two purposes. It both creates new offences relating to terrorism and with this enables the proliferation of narratives of this terrorism as a new and unknown threat that demands new and unheard-of strategies of response, and it provides concrete methods for extending the power of the state and disrupting established norms of legality.

The most famous instances of this remain the USA PATRIOT Act (an acronym standing for the Orwellian phrase 'Uniting and Strengthening America by Providing Appropriate Tools Required to Intercept and Obstruct Terrorism) and the anti-terrorism measures passed in the UK. The PATRIOT Act was passed with extreme haste on 26 October 2001. The sense of emergency allowed for little scrutiny of the 342-page bill. Key elements of the Act have been: to allow the FBI to investigate US citizens even without probable cause if it is for 'intelligence purposes'; to jail non-citizens on suspicion; to allow detention without charge or trial through six-month increments that can be extended indefinitely; to expand the definition of terrorism to include so-called domestic terrorism and so submit political organisations to surveillance, wiretapping and criminalisation for political campaigning; to extend the ability of law enforcement agencies to conduct secret searches, telephone and internet surveillance and to have access to highly personal medical, financial, mental health and student records (for an analysis of its implementation, see Wong, 2007). The Act grants extensive discretion to law enforcement agencies and is reminiscent of previous highly controversial campaigns against political dissent such as COINTELPRO (see Newton, 1996).

Like some other states, initial responses of the British to 9/11 reworked legislation that had been developed with other social demons in mind. The 2001 Act was an adaptation of earlier phases of discussion that had sought to contain the perceived threat of the anti-globalisation movement and other protest groups. Entitled the Anti-Terrorism, Crime and Security Act 2001 (ATCSA), this act cobbled together a range of disparate objectives. These included: cutting terrorist funding; collecting and sharing counterterrorist information across government departments and agencies; streamlining immigration procedures (that is, making deportation easier); ensuring the security of the nuclear and aviation industries and of dangerous substances; extending police powers; meeting international counterterrorism obligations. In effect, the key outcome of this legislation was the detention without trial of a number of foreign nationals. These were men who were deemed to be a risk to national security but who were never brought to trial and who did not know of the allegations made against them. This aspect of the law was overturned by a House of Lords Judicial Committee ruling that such powers were incompatible with articles of the European Convention on Human Rights relating to the right to liberty, and the right to freedom from discrimination. The committee also considered such powers to be discriminatory as they applied only to foreign nationals (see CAMPACC, 2004). In response, new legislation was passed, the Prevention of Terrorism Act 2005, which instituted a system of control orders that applied equally to UK nationals and non-nationals. In practice, the control order scheme has operated as a system of house arrest and has caused severe hardship for vulnerable individuals and their families (Gillan and Al Yafai, 2005). A number of suspects have absconded under the scheme and others have returned home to dangerous regimes rather than continue to place their families under such strain.

In order to maintain the sense of emergency, the UK has continued to develop new phases of anti-terrorism law. The Terrorism Act 2006 had been floated before the 7/7 (7 July 2005) bombings in London, but took on a new urgency after this event. This act extends the conception of anti-terrorist activity to such an extent that its provisions appear to institute a version of thought crime. The key provisions include the following new offences:

- Acts Preparatory to Terrorism
- Encouragement to Terrorism defined as to directly or indirectly incite or encourage others to commit acts of terrorism, including the glorification of terrorism, where this may be understood as encouraging the emulation of terrorism.
- Dissemination of Terrorist Publications, applying both to publications that encourage terrorism, and those that provide assistance to terrorists.

- Terrorist training offences including giving or receiving training in terrorist techniques or attendance at a place of terrorist training.

These provisions have been highly contested by civil liberties and academic groups and others (see Chakrabarti and Crossman, 2007). The inclusion of vaguely defined speech crimes and prohibitions against distributing written documents raises obvious difficulties for policing and the exercise of democratic freedoms. As well as these new offences, the Act extends existing police powers, giving police wider powers to search any property owned or controlled by a terrorist suspect, the ability to proscribe groups that glorify terrorism, and the ability to detain suspects for up to 28 days.

Both US and UK legislation have been framed to increase the discretion of law enforcement agencies and to create police powers that erode the rights of suspects and limit accountability to the wider public. It is for these reasons, presumably, that Egypt, infamous for violating human rights, can claim in response to criticisms of proposals for new anti-terrorism laws that they are based on similar legislation in a number of countries including the US (Amnesty International, 2007). Across the world, repressive measures now are justified through an appeal to the War on Terror and the need to combat international terrorism by any unsavoury means necessary.

For some regions, this process has been no more than a reinvigoration of existing repressive legislation. Malaysia and Singapore have diverted existing laws allowing lengthy detention without charge or trial from the previous ghoul of communism to the new monster of international terrorism. The outcome has been to consolidate and extend the power of the state to persecute political activists in the name of societal security. El Salvador uses anti-terrorist measures to criminalise peaceful protest against cuts in public services. Australia has instituted its own approach to detention or house arrest without trial. Russia continues well-worn repressive practices, including gagging the media, but now justifies such actions as necessary to the battle against terrorism.

Overall, the linking thread through these different approaches to anti-terrorism legislation has been to extend the authority, discretion and non-scrutibility of the state. In practice, such legislative developments enable the targeting of particular groups and communities without any explicit naming of target groups in law. These are not the old-fashioned race laws of old-fashioned racist states. Instead this is a championing of authoritarianism with a liberal face that can be deployed for any racialised or other local struggle.

The legitimisation of an arbitrary implementation of state powers and an acceptance that an unexplained discretion is a necessary and even welcome component of state authority, in an echo of Theweleit's account of the seductive appeal of the secrecy in authoritarian government, creates a localised version of the endless war at home. Just as international terrorism takes the role of an elusive evil that requires ongoing military aggression, domestic security in a range of locations becomes a project of escalating state discretion and force in which calls for democratic scrutiny are derided as helping the terrorists.

The backlash against multiculturalism and imagining terrorist threats

I want to argue that the emergence of an expansionary militarism from the US and its allies infects the conduct of civilian life within these and other nations. This infection builds on previous practices of racialised policing – but with an expansion of targets and an adaptation of the legitimising narrative. Racial myths evolve so that the demonised figure of the 'dangerous black man' becomes the 'dangerous brown man', an adaptation of earlier racist mythologies that may refer to the same groups of men but that enables the inclusion of more recent racialised anxieties. This is a process that continues the influence of US-defined racial politics on other parts of the world – the cultural representation of dangerous blackness in various parts of the world has been shaped by US culture and politics, and similarly the inclusion of dangerous brownness in this formulation echoes shifts in US racial politics, both at home and internationally (Winant, 2001). Importantly, there is a shift to include new communities and develop racial myths for new circumstances. In the process, there is a concerted campaign to suggest that 'race' is no longer the issue and that those who previously suffered racism are now with us (as opposed to against us).

The shift from what I am describing as 'black' to 'brown' myths is centred around the implied dangers of non-western cultures. There is a reworking of long-running racist myths – so the black rapist becomes the brown man from a backward and misogynistic culture, anti-feminist, sexually frustrated by traditional culture, addicted to honour killing and viewing women as tradable objects (for a summary of some of these ideas, see Abbas, 2007). Such a narrative represents a further development of the take-up of anti-essentialism as a defence of racism – the proposition that identities are based on cultures and that cultures are separate and absolutely different enables all kinds of terrible things to be said and, sadly, believed. This is a language of racism that has learned to disavow the terms of 'race' in order to relegitimise racist practises (for a discussion of this so-called cultural racism see Taylor and Spencer, 2004). It is this shift that I am characterising as the refocusing on brown men – with 'brown' here signifying a difference that can be depicted as cultural, non-essential, beyond the horrific histories of violence against Africans and yet enabling a continuance of the link between bodies and social meaning. None of this means that old-fashioned anti-blackness has disappeared (Bashi, 2004). However, I do think the take-up of an active language of anti-racism has altered the public framing of racist activity and that the legitimating narratives of racism, in particular of state racisms, reach for terms that can at once maintain the effects of racial categorisation while refusing the salience of the term 'race'.

Dangerous brown men on our streets

Cultural analyses of the histories of western racisms have uncovered the centrality of the process of making the racialised body excessively visible (Hall, 1997; Gilman, 1985). This repetitive visualisation and visual marking have been an important technique of othering, from the demonisation of Jewish populations across Europe (Gilman, 1991) to the apparently ongoing fixation with the black body (Doy, 2000) to the titillating imaginary of Orientalist exotica (Lewis, 1996). These are conceptions of 'race' that foreground what can be seen, with this visual coding standing in for a wider narrative of what can be understood. Central to these visually triggered understandings is the role of sexuality. This is an important aspect of what is regarded as so visually conspicuous. The racialised other in a range of settings has been presented as grotesquely and excessively physicalised, with this alleged physicality sliding easily into a slur about the sexual behaviours, predilections and prowess of such groups (McLintock, 1993; Gilman, 1985, 1991).

Such mythologies have shaped the representation of black men. Images of the suffering and/or hyperphysicalised black body have circulated to reinforce allegations of animality, bodily unreason and lack of civilisation. A variety of commentators have suggested that the more recent saleability of images of black bodies in the global market-place retains the traces of this biologistic dehumanisation (Collins, 1995; hooks, 1992). Analyses of the playing out of such cultural myths through techniques of state racism have pointed to the work done by these conceptions of black physicality in legitimising police violence and punitive treatment through education, welfare and prison systems (Gooding-Williams, 1993; Neubeck and Casanave, 2001). Racist accounts of the supposed nature of blackness are not peripheral to the hard realities of how powerful institutions subdue black people.

What I am describing as the shift from dangerous black men to dangerous brown men in popular mythologies that legitimise state racism and authoritarianism builds on these histories of constraining the hypervisible black body. However I also want to suggest that this is a slightly different twist in the development of a culture of global racism.

Of course the move from black to brown targets of vilification is somewhat illusory. The populations under scrutiny and attack span the identities of 'black', 'brown' and beyond. What I am arguing is that the conduct of the War on Terror has given rise to renewed techniques of state racism in a variety of locations and this reinvigorated campaign has drawn on distinct mythologies of race and culture.

In terms of repressive techniques, this culturally sensitive version of state racism very much continues the strategies of earlier times. However, the mythology of difference that accompanies these actions is distinct. On the whole, this is not a narrative of racism that centres on such familiar tropes as physicality or hypersexuality.

Instead the fixation on Muslim bodies takes a somewhat different form. It is not the Muslim body that populates global media culture or that serves as the canvass across which national and transnational anxieties can be staged. Within European nations Muslim bodies have entered public consciousness as entities that are too veiled, too bearded, too covered. It is this refusal to participate in the public cultures of commodified physicality that marks out the Muslim body in this popular imagining. I am not suggesting that this is a new phenomenon. Fascination with the body that is veiled or hidden has been a well-documented element of Orientalist fantasy (DelPlato, 2002).

However this fixation has been with the veiled female body. The story of Orientalist titillation has been that these delectable women are hidden from the world by killjoy menfolk who wish to control women's movement (Grosrichard, 1998; Alloula, 1986). The implication of this telling is that women desire physicality, exposure and libidinous release, and this is why men feel compelled to contain women's visibility and movement.

In this narrative there is no implication that Muslims or other 'orientals' are without desire. If anything, these myths are echoes of the race-science-inspired stories of black animality and sexual excess. The East that is characterised by purdah and harems is a place overrun by libidinous drives and licentious physical excess. The fact that such activity is hidden only heightens the fascination (Lewis, 2004). At no point in these Orientalist accounts of Eastern practices of bodily constraint is it implied that the Orient refuses a sexual freedom that is enjoyed by the West. If anything, it is the East that is portrayed as consumed by sex and, unable to exercise the discipline of western manners, must resort to more substantial constraints.

The claim that the War on Terror is being fought to defend the rights of women calls upon a version of this mythology. These are women who must be liberated from the brutality of men who use culture as a pretext for barbarism. Few would question the horror of the Taliban regime for the women and men of Afghanistan. However, the rationale for military intervention used here is based on the belief that the women of Afghanistan and other Muslim nations wish to enter a freedom that is demonstrated by physical openness.

The recent hysteria in Europe that has surrounded issues of veiling reveals a fury at the idea that any woman might choose to cover herself. It appears that such an internalisation of the need for feminine modesty presents a different kind of affront to supposedly western sensibilities (Atasoy, 2006; Thomas, 2006; for a groundbreaking account of the politics of the veil, see Mernissi, 1992). Despite the extensive debate about multiculturalism and the status of women, it is the assertion of cultural identity by Muslim women in the diaspora that has enraged self-styled liberal critics. The often-repeated argument is that such an acceptance of constraints on their appearance and movement by some women endangers the ability of all women in that society to exercise such freedoms (for a review of some European examples of this view, see Fekete, 2006). The fact that until very recently feminists questioned notions of freedom that demanded that women become (even more) sexualised but not empowered has fallen out of public debate (for an overview of some of these debates, see Segal, 1994).

Throughout all of this, the male Muslim body has remained intangible. It is the ephemera of beards and clothing that indicate its difference. There are few public portrayals of this form of physicality (for a welcome collection analysing representations of Muslim masculinity, see Ouzgane, 2006). In this, there is a racism quite distinct from the obsessive and intensive objectification of African bodies that informs European racisms. This is the process that bell hooks identifies when she writes, 'The black body has always received attention within the framework of white supremacy, as racist/sexist iconography has been deployed to perpetuate notions of innate biological inferiority' (hooks, 1994, 127).

Against this, she characterises black liberatory politics as mounting a 'counter hegemonic discourse of the body' (127). Black peoples have learned to fight through and with discourses of the body because racist cultures have been so over-invested in racist conceptions of black physicality. Whether this fight takes the form of a self-conscious repression of all bodily expression or of a parodic celebration of bodily excess, black diasporic identities have been articulated through a relation to the body.

Although recent demonisations of Muslim peoples also build on many centuries of varying contact, antagonism and competition, the image of the Muslim body is less central in this history (Armour, 2002; Armstrong, 1994). However, I do want to argue that the War on Terror has heralded a new visibility for the Muslim body, albeit through various techniques of indirect disclosure and, of course, for racist ends. This is the discussion of the next chapter.

It may be more accurate to describe some of *these events* as emerging from a racialised state as opposed to the racist state itself. The culturalism that has come to influence a range of state practices in the US and Europe inserts a version of racial categorisation into liberal conceptions of proper state working. These developments represent, of course, the outcome of complex struggles for recognition, patronage and routes to fair treatment by different communities and the resulting take-up of various local understandings of the need to consider cultural identity as a component of citizenship and entitlement. However, an additional consequence of these struggles has been the insertion of an everyday version of cultural difference talk that can come to racialise any social situation (for a review of debates about racialisation, see Solomos and Murji, 2005).

The relatively rapid construction of an everyday mythology of 'what Muslims are like' – including detailed narratives about 'their' purported beliefs, histories, social habits and alleged proclivity for violence – builds on this popular familiarity with culturalist accounts of identity and behaviour (for some examples, see Rippin, 2005; Khan, 2003; Lewis, 2004). In a context where explicit racism has ceased to be respectable and where the allegation of racism is regarded as a profound personal slur, the take-up of complex culturalist accounts of difference enables racist antagonisms to be voiced in a different and seemingly legitimate manner.

Whereas 'race' as physical identifier continues to be naturalised and it is on these terms that 'racism' is bad, irrational and unfair, because people cannot help the colour of their skin, the objectionable behaviour and values of other groups is presented as legitimate justification for discriminatory treatment and antagonism.

The various statements that are used to present this position, including government and policy pronouncements, media representations and a range of everyday conversational statements of varying status, tend to be structured to refute the accusation of racism while presenting the legitimacy of unequal treatment or of antagonism to a group (for examples see Koch and Smith, 2006; Khalaf, 2005; for a critical analysis, see Carr, 2006). I am indebted to the analysis of Roger Hewitt in his work on white backlash to multiculturalism for this formulation. Hewitt collates and analyses a series of responses to racist attacks and murders among white groups in particular demonised areas of south London and finds that such utterances contribute to a complex and shared counternarrative about the racist character of the incidents and the role and status of white inhabitants of the area. Overall he finds that there is a shared narrative circulating that asserts that these acts of violence were not motivated by racism and that whites suffer similar levels of racist attack by other groups but that this is not recognised by public authorities or the media. Hewitt summarises the term 'counter-narrative' as 'having the appearance of being proffered in response to a previous story or stories, and of anticipating further narrative moves by others' (Hewitt, 2005, 57).

He goes on to explain the role of such strategies in more general race-related discursive production:

> What specifically characterised race-related discursive production during the second half of the twentieth century was that it was increasingly *dialogic*, in being not only inter-textual (having reference, meaning and resonance within a *corpus* of discursive material) but in being fundamentally demonstrative of its own relation to that corpus. Race-related utterances increasingly *addressed* their discursive 'others' and not uncommonly in agonistic forms. This Bakhtinian dimension was increasingly evident as multiculturalist discourse gradually established its legitimacy and prominence. Race-related discourse of all political hues from the 1960s onwards was redolent with alternate and pre-existing voices as it strove to counter the process of unwelcome attribution. Race-related *narrative* was also frequently party to this kind of conversation. (Hewitt, 2005, 72)

The various disavowals of racism that occur in the name of the War on Terror and the related activity of reclaiming state racism as a legitimate response to dangerous differences of belief and culture could be seen as embodying a wider 'backlash' against the analytic status of race and racism as structuring forces in society. Instead, the rhetoric of us and them portrays this new battle of ideas as rooted in differences of values, beliefs and ways of life. If the other is hiding their adherence to a demonic, violent and destructive culture and set of beliefs, it is not racist to use the surveillance and categorisation techniques of a modern state to limit the threat that this poses. We are back to deciphering bodies, but now in order to discern adherence to these dangerous beliefs.

Religious identity occupies a different status to ideas of 'race', and there have been claims from different quarters that religion is the new race and that ideas of social justice should be reconsidered in the light of this shift (Modood, 1992; Gottschalk, 2007). For those wishing to defend and represent religious minorities, this claim is framed to extend demands for social equality to include extended rights to religious freedom and recognition and a linking of social and cultural rights. For others, the same claim is presented to argue that racism has been eliminated precisely because it was recognised to be an unnecessary and irrational social evil but that antagonism towards the practices and values of religious minorities is not and cannot be racism because religion is an issue of belief and free will. Seeking to accommodate the beliefs and practices of minorities in the name of equality is a bad thing for society, because some beliefs and practices make bad things happen and are bad for society.

The continual return to the alleged status of women in Islam and/or in the conception of those professing various strands of political Islam could be seen to represent one process of counternarrative. In implicit, and sometimes explicit, response to the allegation that Muslim minorities are marginalised and face social exclusion in western societies, a counter-claim is made that alleges that these groups cannot expect equality when their own cultural practices deny equality to women. This claim suggests that the social ills faced by Muslim communities are not discrimination on the grounds of religion or race, but are an outcome of other groups' proper disapproval of Muslim accounts of the status of women. As such beliefs are a cultural choice, unlike the naturalised and absolute difference of physicalised conceptions of race, Muslims should change their unpleasant ways in order to gain social acceptance and equality.

There are similar implications in statements about purported Muslim attitudes to sexuality, personal freedom and allegiance to state and nation. Therefore counternarratives include the suggestions that granting equal treatment to Muslims would entail condoning discrimination against lesbian, gay, bisexual and trans people and a general unleashing of sexual repression against all; that Islam denies personal liberty and therefore any accommodation with Muslim communities would lead to an erosion of personal freedom for all; that Islam demands a transnational and mutual allegiance between Muslims that overrides the claim of any national law or allegiance and therefore Muslims must be scrutinised and persecuted if national security is to be defended.

At the heart of each of these narratives is the assertion that unequal treatment is not only justifiable, it is necessary for the greater good. In the process, racism is resurrected as a respectable and also necessary practice, but now on the grounds of the dangers of insurmountable cultural difference. The demonisation of Muslims serves as a model through which to rework racial difference as a matter of threatening cultural difference and the need to preserve social goods such as women's rights, sexual freedom and personal liberty. Thus, while old-fashioned physicalised racism is derided, yet another new cultural racism emerges to explain the misfortunes of minority communities in the labour market, criminal justice and education systems and at the hands of their neighbours as an outcome of their own illiberal, repressive and discriminatory culture which makes it impossible for them to integrate with the more progressive majority culture and leads to their self-segregation. Muslims are the most identified focus of such narratives, but similar allegations transfer easily to other groups who face disadvantage.

At the same time as the shift in popular racist mythologies calls upon earlier tropes of the sexually predatory other, representations of political/religious extremism imply a refusal of westernised sexual cultures, an alternative set of myths about those who refuse the pleasure-centred commodified 'depravity' of the West. This is portrayed as a highly suspect perversion – one that leads to outbursts of frustrated sexualised violence or, alternatively, that uses sexuality as a tool in a larger ideological battle. The dangerous brown man of the war on terror is a sexualised figure, but this is a different sexualisation from that of the mythically phallic black man. The cultural narrative of terror also relies on an idea of sex: as an explanation for inhuman behaviour; as an extension of the fear of violence; as the narrative that can imaginatively embody the otherwise faceless demons of the War on Terror. The next chapter will consider the workings of sexualised representations in this war.

4

Sexuality in Torture

This chapter will examine accounts of the transnationalisation of torture and abuse in the pursuit of the long war. This examination will include a consideration of reports of detention, extraordinary rendition and the use of torture by the United States and its allies. I look at the cultural myths that enable this machinery of abuse and argue that the transnational circulation of this ugly knowledge plays an important role in the construction of a global public.

The documents considered here present a picture of dehumanisation and abuse that links sexual torture and humiliation with the incorporation of racism and religious attacks into the conduct of physical violence. From these accounts, it appears that the War on Terror continues the long and ugly tradition of torturers from many regimes who have included highly sexualised forms of violence in their repertoire of brutality (for some examples from recent regimes, see Arcel, 1998; Krog, 2000; Mertus, 2000; Oosterhoff et al., 2004). However, in addition, in these examples sexual violations are woven into narratives of cultural disrespect and racism, and the public portrayal of torture focuses on the sexualised impact of such violence, sometimes with the implication that it is this sexual abuse that is the primary affront for people of (a backward, intolerant, repressed) faith.

In the previous chapters there has been a consideration of key elements of the War on Terror, including the representation of sexuality as a marker of freedom or of barbarism, battles over the meaning and location of feminism and the status of women, the construction and circulation of bodies, and the securitisation of everyday space. Through all of these themes, the figure of the terrorist holds a central place. This is the mysterious character that we must understand, identify and destroy. The battles about the meaning of bodies always return to the meaning of the terrorist body.

Sexualised racism and the legitimisation of torture and abuse

Patricia Hill Collins describes the new racism that emerges in the era of globalisation as one that combines an increase in the power of transnational corporations, a decentring of the role of individual governments in shaping a new transnational racism, and a far greater role for ideas purveyed through the media. She describes this last element thus:

> the new racism relies more heavily on the manipulation of ideas within the mass media. These new techniques present hegemonic ideologies that claim that racism is over. They work to obscure the racism that does exist, and they undercut antiracist protest. (Collins, 2005, 54)

The first two themes in Collins's account of this new racism are familiar from more general discussions of the impact of globalisation (Went, 2000; Hedley, 2002). It has become accepted that the forces of global integration are characterised by an increase in corporate power (Korten, 2001) across borders and a decrease in government control over national spaces. It takes only a small leap of imagination or curiosity to suggest that these two trends, however uneven and incomplete, must have an impact on social phenomena such as racism (Chua, 2003).

However the third suggestion goes beyond this easy extension of globalisation theories. There is plenty of work that argues that the growth in reach and influence of the mass media represents another particular and significant theme of our time (Rantanen, 2005; Hjarvard, 2003). However the suggestion that there is a battle of ideas in which the status and existence of racism is under constant question is of another order. Collins describes a world in which the divisions and inequalities of racism grow larger and more intense (for more on globalisation and deepening inequality, see Hurrell and Woods, 1999), yet where the public disavowal of racism becomes louder and more insistent.

Her project is to analyse the particular and intense racisms directed against African-American communities and, to this end, she outlines a range of areas where African-American communities continue to face excessive disadvantage and extreme violence. For Collins this is proof of the urgent need for a reassessment of anti-racist movements and a reclaiming of the central and unique experience of African-Americans in the framing of such movements. There may be other communities who also feel that their experience is and should be central to any consideration of a renewed anti-racist politics, in particular because the experience of African-Americans as a non-migrant racialised minority with an extensive history at the heart of the US national formation is not mirrored elsewhere or by other communities and the reinvigorated racisms of our global times clearly mobilise antagonism to a number of groups. However the idea that global racisms are expressed through a concerted denial of the existence of racism in transnational media chimes with key aspects of the War on Terror. This is a central contention of my book: that the War on Terror both operates through the mobilisation of familiar racisms and serves to construct a new global space of racist understanding, where racism is at once decried and endlessly circulated as the unpalatable knowledge that allows membership in the global public.

Is the War on Terror a racist war?

A significant theme in defences of the War on Terror is that it is not racist. President Bush asserted this repeatedly in his public speeches (see, for example, 'Islam is peace, says President', cited in Croft, 2006, 105). Blair echoes the same themes (Blair, 2006). Stuart Croft describes this 'non-racism' in terms of a series of decisive cultural interventions made in the aftermath of 9/11, which include 'the decisive inter-vention ... to (re)construct an idea of equality of treatment of all Americans' (Croft, 2006, 104). The claim that western nations embody global values such as equality has formed an important aspect of the justificatory narrative accompanying the War on Terror.

In Britain, in House of Commons debates in the period after 9/11, speakers from each major political party both pledged their support and sympathy for the US and proclaimed the importance of reaching out to Muslim communities. In the immediate aftermath, Jack Straw, then Foreign Secretary, asserted the inclusive character of the coalition that was being formed:

> Terrorists operate without regard for borders. The fight against terrorism therefore needs to be a global one. Only a true coalition of the civilised world offers a real chance of cutting out that cancer. As we construct that coalition, we will include the Islamic world. No one should be in any doubt: those acts of mass murder have nothing to do with the Islamic faith. (UK, *Hansard*, 14 September 2001, column 620)

In another example of anticipatory counternarrative, Parmjit Dhanda, then a Labour backbencher, pre-empts any complaints from Muslim communities: 'It is particularly important at the moment to reassure the Muslim communities both at home and abroad that we are not at war with Islam. Muslims are not the enemies of the British people' (UK, *Hansard*, 4 October 2001, column 767). Throughout the debate there is an unease with the possible racist implications of these utterances and these actions. David Blunkett, the Home Secretary of the time and someone who later made great play of his refusal to be constrained by liberal complaints, explained the importance of combining initiatives against terrorism with an attention to the situation of minority communities: 'We want to avoid the exploitation of the situation domestically. ... We are endeavouring to unify our community, and to avoid divisions and conflict at the very moment when we need that unity most of all.' (UK, *Hansard*, 15 October 2001, pt 8, column 933).

This, then, is a conflict where key players anticipated the accusation of racism from the outset. After the battles about institutional racism and racial privilege of recent decades (Better, 2002; Bhavnani et al., 2005), the political leaders of western nations have, largely, internalised the lesson that racism is bad. Or, more precisely, that it is bad to be identified as racist. Open and public declarations of racial supremacism are regarded as taboo, the kind of barbarism that our enemies indulge in. As a result, injunctions to join the War on Terror are structured around a double-speak that both constructs a new and monstrous racial enemy and decries racism at every step.

From the outset the interventions in Afghanistan and Iraq have been shaped by a racialised rhetoric. George Bush's famous test –' you are either with us or against us' – splits the world into absolute and incompatible racial teams. If this test appeared to echo the political divides of the Cold War, this was because that ideological contest had itself been transformed into a racialised conflict against a Soviet bloc characterised as innately authoritarian, corrupt, soulless and racially other to the happily diverse individualism of the West (for an account of Cold War cultural representations, see English and Halperin, 1987). The important aspect for our purposes is that a battle of ideas or politics can take on a racialised character if the conflict is understood to be based on an absolute and impassable difference, not of ideas but of being. Bush may describe this as a struggle against evil, but the world clearly understands him to refer to groups of people who are seen to embody this otherness. By the time we have moved on to the accusation that those who harbour terrorists belong to this category of evil, the racial barriers are well established.

For those who believe the War against Terror to be a war against Islam it is significant that Muslim nations are being singled out for violent attack and occupation and that Muslim populations around the world are facing repressive policing. From the outset we have been warned that the War on Terror is unlike any previous conflict. This is a battle that combines old-fashioned invasions of less powerful nations, a suggestion that disguised strangers threaten national security from within, serves as a linking narrative between state repression of minorities in many places including through military means, and a plan to transform global consciousness through the combined means of state surveillance, harassment, abuse and cultural injunction. The outcome of all of this intensive activity is that, whatever the repeated assertions made by key players, most of the world witnesses the War on Terror as a series of attacks on Muslim individuals and communities. While many may agree that the invasions of Afghanistan and Iraq do not constitute a military campaign against the Muslim world, the less newsworthy actions of various nations all confirm the view that 'Muslim' has become a new category of transnational significance in the politics of race.

Spectacularisation as a form of abuse

Accounts of war rape have argued that this crime is designed to terrorise the whole community (Stiglmayer, 1994; Goldstein, 2001). It is this symbolic defilement that is desired. War rape, we have learned, has its own horrific and instrumental logic. It is not an aberration or an extra-military outpouring of lust and violence. This is part of the conduct of war, part of the process that proves war to be inextricably bound to the politics of gender and of race (Chang, 1998; Allen, 1996). War rape is an address to the enemy – 'look at us violate your people, look at us contaminate your stock and make your children ours, look at how helpless you are before our brutality'. Sex has nothing to do with it.

However, in earlier histories of systematic sexual abuse in the pursuit of war, this has remained a secret of the battle zone (for an influential survey of the politics of rape, including war rape, see Brownmiller, 1993). The abused community, all too often under occupation or suffering terrorisation from a stronger enemy force, may live with the knowledge of these abuses. It may be that the purpose is to extend the sense of terror and helplessness to the entire community. However, in previous conflicts, such abuses have been hidden from populations 'back home'.

In the War on Terror, images and accounts of sexualised abuse have formed an integral component of the iconography of the conflict. Some of these are illicit images from infamous instances of abuse at Abu Ghraib. Some are more coded yet unmistakable, such as detainees at Guantánamo being manhandled across the camp, clutching ragged loincloths. The narratives that circulate alongside such images are widely available. The *Washington Post* used its website to publish a series of signed witness statements from detainees who had suffered abuse at Abu Ghraib. Others have collected and published testimony from those detained at Guantánamo (Stafford Smith, 2007; for an account from a former military chaplain, see Yee, 2005). Since their release, Moazzam Begg has published a book documenting his experiences of capture and detention (Begg, 2006) and Asif Iqbal, Ruhal Ahmed and Shafiq Rasul, the so-called Tipton Three, have collaborated on the film *The Road to Guantánamo*. Other British Guantánamo detainees such as Jamal Udeen have given widely publicised interviews to British newspapers and television.

In Britain at least, the debates about detention without trial for foreign nationals accused of terror charges have rehearsed the revelations about torture and sexualised abuse again. Despite the ruling that evidence obtained through torture should not be admissible in a British court (Silverman, 2005; *Guardian*, 2005a), the attempted defence of the use of supposed information derived from torture serves to reiterate that democratic states now view torture as a necessary evil in the battle against international terrorism. All of this makes institutionalised violence and torture an open secret of the long war, a secret revealed both through visualisation and suggestion.

There are several elements to the spectacularisation of the War on Terror. One is the visual record of key events, including iconic instances of abuse, and the circulation of such images via the internet and international media. Linked to this visual recording is the suggestion that this is a war that requires the active demonstration and theatricalisation of power – 'shock and awe'.

This intimidation through images has been answered, perhaps predictably, with the emergence of the gory genre of 'jihadi' videos. Key elements of the visualisation of Guantánamo such as the orange jumpsuits and the hooding of kneeling figures have been replicated in recordings of kidnapped western hostages. At their worst, these recordings have shown the murder of their victims in gruesome and spectacular manner to be broadcast via the internet. The exchange of horrific images has formed a significant component of the larger battle to shape global opinion.

However alongside the relatively explicit calls to make this war visible, other, more coded accounts circulate among the global public. Some of these come from the properly recorded testimony of former detainees and include investigations by human rights organisations, lawyers and journalists. Some come from the writings of those who have been released such as Moazzam Begg's book *Enemy Combatant*. Alongside these accounts other, more fragmented narratives also exist. These are the accounts that former and current detainees and their lawyers and friends have heard but cannot yet substantiate. I want to consider this kind of information as rumour, not because I believe that these claims have no basis, but because I want to argue that the global circulation of racialised rumour serves a central purpose in the cultural project of the War on Terror.

As well as the rumours of secret prisons, secret prisoners and secret abuses, there are parallel rumours from proponents of the War on Terror. These are the rumours about the nature of Arab or Muslim culture; suggestions of the sensitive areas that enrage these communities beyond the grasp of any reasonable response; mobilisations of ideas of cultural difference that transplant the local racialised tensions of western nations onto a global stage and vice versa; most of all that insistent whispering that this is what these people are really like, deep down in their essence.

Rumour has been a highly charged component of other eras of racialised violence. Rumour has been the favoured vehicle to transform racist vendettas into battles for the sexual reputation and honour of white women and, by implication, of the white race (for accounts of famous cases of racist rumour, see Sorensen, 2003; Metress, 2002). More recently, rumour has been the technique that mobilises rival groupings and hardens the battle lines between minorities and between majorities and minorities.

A rumour is not a secret. Rumour is a very public means of communication and the point is not to hide what is being said. I do not think that the transnational audience for the War on Terror is created through the deployment of secrets. This is not a project that seeks to create unity through revelation. Instead this global public is constituted in part through access to knowledge that resists substantiation (Daase and Kessler, 2007).

The famous and over-quoted instance of this is the remark made by Donald Rumsfeld at a Department of Defense news briefing on 12 February 2002:

> As we know, there are known knowns. There are things we know we know. We also know There are known unknowns. That is to say we know there are some things we do not know. But there are also unknown unknowns, the ones we don't know we don't know.

The cultural project of the War on Terror mobilises this sense of unknown unknowns. The unease of this almost-knowledge is a central component of what I have described as the construction of a global public. What follows is an attempt to reveal the workings of the formation through suggestion of this global assembly.

Sexualised racism as a strategy of dehumanisation

In a piece analysing cultural responses to the beating of black motorist Rodney King by Los Angeles police, Elizabeth Alexander argues that the forced visual spectacle of racist violence and battered black bodies creates a painful sense of peoplehood for African-Americans.

> Black bodies in pain for public consumption have been an American spectacle for centuries. This history moves from public rapes, beatings, and lynchings to the gladiatorial arenas of basketball and boxing. In the 1990s, African-American bodies on videotape have been the site on which national trauma – sexual harassment, 'date rape', drug abuse, racial and economic urban conflict, AIDS – has been dramatized. (Alexander, 1994, 92)

This dramatisation plays an important role in the ongoing construction of the national narrative. Alexander is describing the manner in which this spectacle of the black body acts as the emblem and the stage for these various 'traumas'. Sources of anxiety in the national psyche become embodied through these representations of black bodies, and the echo of the spectacle of lynching informs public understandings. Alexander suggests that such images place viewers differently according to their role in the US theatre of race and racism.

> In each of these traumatic instances, black bodies and their attendant dramas are publicly 'consumed' by the larger populace. White men have been the primary stagers and consumers of the historical spectacles I have mentioned, but in one way or another, black people have been looking, too, forging a traumatized collective historical memory which is reinvoked, I believe, at contemporary sites of conflict. (Alexander, 1994, 93)

The suggestion is, I think, that these continual restagings of the black body in pain play a constitutive role in racialising identity in America. The repetitive seeing of these horrors is an important part of assuming racialised identity, of knowing who you are and where you fit in this drama. For the black viewer such images are a reminder of the violent retribution that can await those who refuse the racial hierarchy and an unsettling reminder that this remains the 'meaning' of black bodies. For Alexander this is the bottom line of collective black consciousness in America, but I think the implications of her argument can be stretched to consider the racist display of battered bodies in a transnational context and the role such images play in placing all viewers as participants in a global culture of racism.

My interest is in the conception of unwilling spectatorship that she outlines. I have tried to argue that the cultural project of the War on Terror has operated by addressing global audiences through indirect means. This is not a manner of propaganda that has sought to present explicitly racist messages. The reader/viewer who has become adept at understanding the implied racist message of various communication forms, which I take to be a skill that indicates sufficient familiarity with western/ised media to gain membership of the global public, will recognise the barely hidden racism that pervades the public emanations of the War on Terror. However, the explicit rhetoric of the war has been one that seeks to pre-empt accusations of racism. Instead of explicit triumphalism, this has been a cultural strategy that operates through the leaking of suggestive snippets and rumours. It is the witnessing of a glimpse of horror that places the viewer as participant here. In the process, viewers are warned and disciplined, in part through their own media-literate ability, to imagine what else lies beyond the glimpse that they have seen. This is a specularity that does not offer the pleasures of the gaze. Alexander goes on to revisit well-known slave narratives in order to examine the placing of the un-willing black spectator to racist violence.

She cites the recorded memory of Frederick Douglass as he watches another slave ('an own aunt of mine') whipped, and his phrase 'I felt doomed to be a witness and a participant' (Alexander, 1994, 96; Douglass, 1982, 51) and that of Mary Prince who remembers the violence and resulting death suffered by a pregnant woman slave with the phrase 'I could not bear to think about it; yet it was always present to my mind' (Alexander, 1994, 99; Ferguson, 1987, 57).

The knowledge that comes from this witnessing is painful and haunting. It dooms the viewer to become a participant, to become an interpellant in the bloody scenario, to carry the unwelcome image around as a constant reminder of the precariousness of life and of the horror of human conduct. Alexander uses these ideas to argue that contemporary stagings of the black body serve to discipline black viewers in similar ways, with each symbolic lynching confirming that this is the meaning of blackness to all. The cultural representation of the War on Terror, through both images and rumours, similarly places the viewer/audience as witness and participant doomed to hold such horror present in their minds. The simultaneous denial and propagation of racism suggests both that the project is to subdue dangerous lesser peoples and that we cannot be certain who falls into such a category. Viewers learn both that a ruthless power acts in their name and that this subjection is not limited to any one identifiable group. It is done in our name, but it could be done to us.

Pictures of abuse

The revelation of prisoner abuse at Abu Ghraib would not have produced the same levels of interest and outrage were it not for the photographs taken by those involved. Public discussion has returned again and again to the meaning of those images. At times it seems that there has been an elision between disgust at the abuse and disgust at being made to see such things.

The resurrection of an international and very public debate about the place of torture in the security armoury of legitimate states has, among other things, brought forth the suggestion that the privilege of not acknowledging the horror carried out to protect citizens of liberal states cannot and should not be sustained (see the discussion from contributors to Levinson, 2004). That naïvety is not appropriate for these times of international terrorism, apparently, and the cosseted citizens of liberal nations should begin to appreciate that their freedoms are not innocent.

In this context the shock of seeing what was done in Abu Ghraib is important to how this debate is shaped. In an influential essay, Mark Danner suggests that, 'It is this photography that has let us visualize something of what happened' (Danner, 2004, 6). Danner is not one of those arguing that we must all see this abuse because we are indebted to those who carry out such horrors to protect our freedoms. However, he does suggest that, despite the considerable information available about abuse of War on Terror detainees in Iraq and elsewhere, photographs bring another level of engagement and awareness in the viewer. With photographs we can visualise things that previously were only heard. Unlike the drawn-out rhythm of narrative accounts, the image can force the viewer to take in the whole story in an instant. Once you have looked it is too late to stop it. Even after you have turned away, the memories and implications of the image keep unravelling in your head, adding to the unwelcome knowledge of horror in the world.

In response to those who explain Abu Ghraib as an inexplicable aberration, Danner reads a training pamphlet from the Marine Corps on cultural sensitivities in Iraq as evidence that the abuses at Abu Ghraib are designed to be a particular and intense affront to Muslims and/or Arabs.

> The *public* nature of the humiliation is absolutely critical; thus the parading of naked bodies, the forced masturbation in front of female soldiers, the confrontation of one naked prisoner with one or more others, the forcing together of naked prisoners in 'human pyramids'. And all of this was made to take place in full view not only of foreigners, men and women, but also of that ultimate third party: the ubiquitous digital camera with its inescapable flash, there to let the detainee know that the humiliation would not stop when the act itself did but would be preserved into the future in a way that the detainee would not be able to control. (Danner, 2004, 33)

Here again is an indication that the lessons of cultural understanding have been redeployed for repressive ends. The knowledges of multiculturalism have become part of the military endeavour. Knowing how people might feel, how to judge their values and responses – knowing how to walk in their shoes, as injunctions to mutual tolerance and understanding would have it – all become an additional strategy to incite terror.

> These are all forms of abuse that would damage any human being, but leading naked Iraqi males around on dog leashes and covering their heads with women's underwear look like techniques designed specifically in order to attack the prisoner's identity and values. (Gray, 2004, 49)

There is a culturalist rationale to the sexualised repression carried out in the name of the War on Terror. This has been widely discussed in a range of literature seeking to uncover the particular cultural construction of US security services attitudes to Islam (Hersh, 2004a; Puar, 2005a). At the same time, the claim that this is a war to defend the rights of women relies on the more muted assertion that our enemy is the enemy of women. In both instances, the representation of the gender and sexual politics of Islam (and others) continues to perform a central role in defining the terms of this conflict.

There are a number of competing strands in this phenomenon. There is, of course, the repeated suggestion that political Islam veers towards the repression of women, sexual minorities and personal freedom (Mazarr, 2007). In the hands of violent and authoritarian men these cultural tendencies also become more violent and authoritarian. To oppose this brutal expression of culture is to defend the universal goods of freedom and rights for all, and this opposition is presented as a duty for all justice-loving people. Not to stand against such oppression is presented as tacit assent. In this chain of association, anti-Islamic sentiment becomes a mark of allegiance to so-called western values of freedom and rights, including importantly the rights of women and sexual minorities.

At the same time, such culturalist arguments are themselves an outcome of a version of cultural sensitivity. This is Orientalism in a literal sense – the deployment of cultural knowledge of the East in order to serve the interests of the western observer (see Said, 2003 for a consideration of Orientalist tactics in the War on Terror). Culture becomes a static attribute that is held by the other and which can be known and used as a tool of subjugation. In the process, the suggestion that it is 'they' who are addicted to a barbaric, irrational and sex-hating culture is reaffirmed.

None of what I write here is to suggest that no one is mobilising young men against the sexual and other depravities of the West or that it is untrue to claim that some are agitated about the apparent moral failures of western life. My interest is in examining why this particular issue becomes so central in western public understandings of cultural division and in justifications for the long war. Can this really be what is at stake in all that serious talk about defending 'our' way of life?

When torture is not a secret

The thing about prisoner abuse in occupied Iraq is that it is not a secret. The Americans in the Abu Ghraib photographs are not trying to hide anything. Quite the opposite – they are recording these events for their own pleasure, as souvenirs of these occasions. If the world was shocked, which I doubt, it was at this too cheerful and too guileless snap-happiness – the 'wait a minute, let me get in the shot, thumbs up to camera' grins on faces that are all too easy to identify. Everyone now knows that the powerful abuse their power, but we expect this to be hidden, as if there is a shame to these crimes of which we all know. Open display is confusing – at once a throwback to earlier methods of demonstrating absolute power (Sawday, 1995) and an unsettling indication that we are somewhere new. Jagbir Puar reminds us not to pretend surprise at the Abu Ghraib scandal:

> The violence performed at Abu Ghraib is not an exception to, nor an extension of, imperialist occupation. Rather, it works in concert with proliferating modalities of force, an indispensable part of the so-called shock-and-awe campaign blueprinted by the Israelis on the backs of Palestinian corpses. Bodily torture is but one element in a repertoire of techniques of occupation and subjugation. (Puar, 2005a, 13)

The War on Terror makes me confused and uneasy, uneasy in that deep way that makes you wake with a sick feeling and wish you could claw back the vague sense of well-being that seems to slip away as consciousness returns. Most of the time I feel afraid, that these inescapable cross-border powers are designed to terrorise me and mine, fear that there is nowhere left to run. The experience of being protected is turning me into a nervous wreck.

Others beside Danner have suggested that the visual recording of the humiliations at Abu Ghraib is itself a central element of the abuse.

Seymour Hersh, in his extensive reporting of prisoner abuse, suggests that a Washington elite became infatuated with a version of cultural anthropology that persuaded them that sexual humiliation was a central lever to destroying Arab resistance and sense of self (Hersh, 2004a). As a result, dated academic work such as the 1973 book *The Arab Mind* by Raphael Patai was transformed into a central organising document and viewed as an insight into the essential and timeless character of the 'Arab'. Jagbir Puar discusses this process, and forcefully critiques its conclusions, in particular challenging the contention that being forced to simulate 'gay' sex is a particular humiliation for Muslims, a contention she finds to be voiced both by CIA spokespeople and liberal writers and activists. Popular commentary in Britain also echoed this view that Muslims have particular and stringent taboos in relation to sexuality and, therefore, that to be pictured suffering sexual abuse represented the most extreme of humiliations (Dodd, 2004; Vallely, 2004; Leigh, 2004). Some have suggested that the pictures, in fact, were taken for the purposes of state-sponsored blackmail – a lever to persuade detainees to become informants (Hersh, 2004a).

I am not so sure about any of this. Yes, of course there are cultural particularities for any community – and I suppose that the horror of torture can mobilise a knowledge of these particularities. I also think that there is something strangely sexualised about the War on Terror and some of its most iconic abuses. However, such sexualisation is not a new phenomenon and is not unique to this oddly nebulous conflict. Sexual abuse has formed part of the degrading repertoire of torturers throughout history (Greenberg, 2006, 5). Yet something about the (non)revelation of the various tortures employed in the pursuit of the War on Terror is unsettling in a different way. Despite everything I know about the horrors that human beings have inflicted upon each other, learning about the conduct of the War on Terror has brought a new level of fear. Although there is a well-documented history of the US sponsoring human rights abuses (see for example, Kiernan 1978/ 2005), I am finding it hard to understand the particular formation of abuse that is emerging now. I expect power to be abused for instrumental ends. However horrific and indefensible, I expect to be able to make sense of what is happening – people are tortured for a point, usually to augment the power that abuses them. For a military power, masquerading as a force of global liberation, to present torture as an open secret and a security necessity not only to the occupied but also to their domestic audience seems to bring something new to the repertoire of state terror.

Why pictures?

At the end of 2005 the newspapers were full of allegations about the 'extraordinary renditions' of terrorist suspects – the outsourcing of interrogation and torture by the US in a process that transports detainees around the world to locations where they could face torture from those working in alliance with the US (for some examples, see Mayer, 2005; Jeffery and Ryan, 2005; *Guardian*, 2005b).

In response, at the outset of an official visit at the close of 2005 to build bridges with Europe, US Secretary of State, Condoleezza Rice, delivered a carefully constructed statement in order to answer concerns that CIA-sponsored torture flights were using European airports for such transportation. Her carefully prepared statement merits close attention – as a public declaration of the workings of the War on Terror and as a lesson in navigating, or perhaps bypassing, international law.

Rice is careful to defend US conduct, but her defence is strangely formulated. She denies that the US could be involved in transporting people for the purpose of torture – but at the same time seems to suggest that in such extreme circumstances extreme responses may be acceptable:

> One of the difficult issues in this new kind of conflict is what to do with captured individuals who we know or believe to be terrorists. The individuals come from many countries and are often captured far from their original homes. Among them are those who are effectively stateless, owing allegiance only to the extremist cause of transnational terrorism. Many are extremely dangerous. And some have information that may save lives, perhaps even thousands of lives. The captured terrorists of the 21st century do not fit easily into traditional systems of criminal or military justice, which were designed for different needs. We have to adapt. Other governments are now also facing this challenge. (Rice, 2005)

This section of the speech brings together some key aspects of the conduct of the War on Terror. The world now knows that a large number of people are being detained by the United States – at Guantánamo, in Afghanistan, in Iraq, in secret prisons across the world (Grey, 2006). The often-repeated justification has been that the US is under unprecedented attack and that these unfortunate men, women and children are imprisoned in order to protect America and its citizens. As Rice argues elsewhere in the same speech, this is the first responsibility of government. However, as she admits here, these judgements may be as much a matter of belief as of knowledge. The individuals concerned are portrayed as displaced already – far from home, perhaps without effective citizenship of anywhere. However, this misfortune, far from being an occasion for compassion, becomes the issue that makes a person endlessly vulnerable. Those who are 'effectively stateless' – a term that encompasses those without citizenship due to, say, refugee status, those who belong to states that are not in a position to exercise their sovereignty or protect their citizens, and those who are citizens of states who do not wish to protect their citizens, particularly against the United States – are doubly stigmatised. It is worth noting that the US is not a signatory to the 1954 UN Convention Relating to the Status of Stateless Persons, a convention designed to ameliorate the particular vulnerability of those without state affiliation. The effectively stateless come to embody the new and diffuse enemy imagined through the War on Terror – collapsing together the new demons of failing states, transnational terrorism and highly mobile extremists who have no allegiance to any government and are therefore immune to the usual pressure points of international diplomacy (Cooper, 2004). At the same time, to be effectively stateless is to fall outside the protections of international law, because without an effective state to protect their interests, there is no one to know, care or ask questions about these people. As Rice admits here, such detainees are not held in accordance with military or civilian justice, but face adaptations that have been developed for the War on Terror. What is this if not an admission that international law is being disregarded?

The careful and convoluted defence offered by Condoleezza Rice demonstrates that rendition is regarded as a defensible tactic: there is no danger that this admission will return to haunt public servants pursuing their duty in relation to the War on Terror. 'Rendition' is defended as a legal and longstanding practice (Priest, 2004; ABC News Online, 2005). However, when torture is denied alongside this defence of rendition, everyone knows that torture is taking place. The only question is whether the US or its allies can be held accountable for enabling and instigating this torture – not morally, which is beyond question, but through any meaningful legal or diplomatic channel. There is little attempt to hide what is being done, only to deny culpability.

The War on Terror has brought a series of such non-revelations: horror upon horror, all of which are admitted, yet presented as necessary. Abu Ghraib and Baghram, Guantánamo and Belmarsh, extraordinary rendition and the strange oxymoron of the officially ghosted prisoner – all of it revealed to the public with the defence of combating terrorism (see Begg, 2006, Grey, 2006). John Pilger argues that this is the distinction between the occupation of Iraq and his earlier experience of reporting from the Vietnam war:

> The difference today is that the truth of the equally atrocious Anglo-American invasion of Iraq is news. Moreover, leaked Pentagon documents make clear that torture is widespread in Iraq. Amnesty International says it is 'systematic'.
>
> And yet, we have only begun to identify the unspeakable element that unites the invasion of Vietnam with the invasion of Iraq. This element draws together most colonial occupations, no matter where or when. It is the essence of imperialism, a word only now being restored to our dictionaries. It is racism. (Pilger, 2004)

The fictions of 'race' enable the cruelties and carnage of imperial adventures – because these people are not like us, are not people at all, and their otherness proves that they are lesser, unworthy, dangerous, and to be contained by any means possible. My broad sympathy has been with a materialist account of racism and the various debates that suggest that racism is tied to concrete interests and economic relations (for example, see Miles, 1989). These are ways of thinking that make racism make sense, of a sort – because in these accounts racism bears some relation to real events and interests and represents both a structure of power and a method of securing the interests of the racially privileged. In the face of concerted efforts from many quarters to depict racism as a universal weakness of human nature, I think it is important to defend a structural account of racism and to retain an analysis of the conduct of power. I do think that there are elements of the War on Terror that are, obviously, instrumental in the manner of other colonial wars; that there is a battle for resources and a demonisation of the occupied population that enables expropriation and occludes history and international law (for a discussion of this, see

Klein et al., 2005). It seems obvious that the peoples of Iraq, Afghanistan and other places are being transformed into 'natives', with all the misfortune that term implies. I take this to be one aspect of what Samir Amin describes as the division of the world (again) into 'masters' and 'natives':

> this 'Master Race' has the right to conquer 'the living space' deemed necessary, while the very existence of other peoples is tolerated only if it does not constitute a threat to the ambitions of those called upon to be 'masters of the world'. Hence, in the eyes of the Washington establishment, we have all become 'redskins', that is, peoples that have a right to exist only in so far as we do not obstruct the expansion of the transnational capital of the United States. (Amin, 2004, 77)

However, I also think that the War on Terror, alongside more obviously instrumental ends, is motivated by unacknowledged sexual anxieties – and this idea offers a critique of the rationalist view that portrays racism as the pursuit of group interests. I am trying to comprehend both the material basis of the unorthodox forms of economic and military expansion that constitute the War on Terror and the more fantastical sexualised narratives that surround this seemingly endless endeavour. Whatever the objectives of the War on Terror, it is clearly more than a simple expression of material interests. Introducing the concept of an unacknowledged and violent expression of sexuality allows us to consider the ways in which racism, including the racism of the War on Terror, may be out of control.

Scholars of sexuality have sought to argue that 'sex' cannot be understood as a normal or natural act (Weeks, 1985; Adams, 1997; Fuss, 1990). Despite the claims of those wishing to champion biology, the body does not ensure that we all engage in standardised and reproductively centred sex (Califia, 1994). Desire is diffuse and unpredictable, and one person's ecstasy may be the cause of indifference or disgust to another. The intention here is not to propose and defend some normative vision of sex that is corroded by sexual abuse. However, I do want to build on the insight that sexual abuse and violence should not be understood as sex, or, at least, not primarily as sex (for an account of how survivors' testimony has shaped our understanding of sexual abuse, see Plummer, 1995). Instead I want to argue that the infliction of sexual humiliation as a component of the institutionalised torture and abuse of detainees in the War on Terror is a distortion of the intimacy of a sexual relationship.

This is the suggestion made by David Luban in a discussion of sexualised torture and the abusive distortion of interpersonal intimacy in the relationship between torturer and victim:

> Torture aims … to strip away from its victim all the qualities of human dignity that liberalism prizes. It does this by the deliberate actions of a torturer, who inflicts pain one-on-one, up close and personal, in order to break the spirit of the victim – in other words, to tyrannize and dominate the victim. The relationship between them becomes a perverse parody of friendship and intimacy: intimacy transformed into its inverse image, where the torturer focuses on the victim's body with the intensity of a lover, except that every bit of that focus is bent to causing pain and tyrannizing the victim's spirit. At bottom all torture is rape, and rape is tyranny. (Luban, 2006, 38)

The distortion of intimacy that appears to pervade much of the abuse reported from the War on Terror fulfils this account of tyranny, but also adds some racialised elements. The combination of sexual abuse, sexualised violence and defamation of religious objects and scriptures seems to link these affronts along a continuum where cultural knowledges are employed by the torturers in an attempt to heighten their ability to create a tyrannising intimacy. This is a deployment of supposed cultural sensitivity or a kind of corrupted glocalised consciousness – a globalised logic where international powers operate through local cultural scripts to enhance their domination. The fixation on sexual organs and abusive acts of penetration and masturbation, however, goes beyond this to a more old-fashioned and absolute attempt to dehumanise. These acts are reminiscent of the sexualised violence embedded in recent genocides, representing a desire to annihilate the other completely (see Jones, 2006; Mills and Brunner, 2002).

It seems that here the exercise of power and privilege is amplified and reshaped through such illogical and unruly impulses as cultures of sex. However, it also seems that there is something particular in the representation of newsworthy abuse – something that harnesses the out-of-control racism of the War on Terror in order to both pacify and petrify those of us who are being 'protected'.

The Abu Ghraib scandal focused on the publication of incriminating photographs, and the brazenness of the photos has caused as much consternation as what was recorded. The published pictures – and it is known that there are others which have not reached the public – add to the iconography of the War on Terror, an iconography that presents torture as acceptable and comprehensible. We recognise the stylised images: orange jumpsuit and shackles, head hooded with electrodes, cowering from dogs, formations of naked bodies, thumbs-up overseers against posed dehumanised detainees. These are images that represent torture as a series of frozen tableaux: literal snapshots of the torture process. They become emblematic as the moment that can be represented and through this representation stand in for the whole. Elizabeth Dauphinee suggests something similar when she writes, 'As physical pain is seen to destroy the possibility of its own expression in language, the options for representing pain are limited to a range of visual practices that can only ever point to some trace – some visible *cause* that might point to the presence of pain in another' (Dauphinee, 2007, 141). The theatricalised representation of sexual humiliation and abuse functions as this visible cause of pain, and suggests both physical and psychological pain to the viewer.

I am beginning to think that these synecdochal instances are forwarded because of the impact they can have on audiences back home. Look, see, this is what torture looks like. Or, equally, perhaps, look, see, these abuses are unfortunate, but they cannot be mistaken for the unspeakable horror of torture. Either way, what is represented purports to be the instance that holds the meaning of the process – and these instances collapse physical pain, sexual abuse, cultural humiliation, fear and objectification. We, the back-home audience, understand that this iconography alludes to a multi-layered process of dehumanisation.

Narratives of suffering

Verbal testimony from former detainees at Abu Ghraib has been available in the public realm for some time, yet these matter-of-fact narratives have not received the frenzy of attention occasioned by the photographs. In these accounts, the speakers position themselves as witnesses to the photographs – these are the events to be verified, what has been photographed shapes the manner in which evidence is given.

> they told me to lay down on my stomach and they were jumping from the bed onto my back and my legs. And the other two were spitting on me and calling me names, and they held my hands and legs. ... One of the

police was pissing on me and laughing on me. He then released my hands and I want (*sic*) and washed, and then the soldier came back into the room, and the soldier and his friend told me in a loud voice to lie down, so I did that. And then the policeman was opening my legs, with a bag over my head, and he sat down between my legs on his knees and I was looking at him from under the bag and they wanted to do me because I saw him and he was opening his pants, so I started screaming loudly and the other police started hitting me with his feet on my neck and he put his feet on my head so I couldn't scream.' (Detainee 1430, 21 January, *Washington Post*, 2004)

Other testimonies repeat similar catalogues of abuse – brutal beatings, humiliation and threats, the use of disorienting techniques, layer upon layer of dehumanising attacks on the person. There is no one incident in the narrative that provides the climax. The threatened rape is not the ultimate or final abuse – other abuses precede and follow, with little sense of strategic intensification. A number of the incidents in this narrative and others reveal a sexualised element to the abuse, but the sexualised abuse is not the focal moment of the narrative. It is no more or less than another horror to be endured, one more episode in the sequence of horrors.

The narratives give a different sense of the experience of torture. Whereas the frozen image suggests a moment of high horror – an emblematic abuse that serves to signify a range of offences that defy representation – the narrative embodies something of the tempo, duration and boring repetition of the suffered abuses:

After they took off my clothes … I saw an American female soldier … in front of me, they told me to stroke my penis in front of her and then they covered my head again, and as I was doing whatever they asked to do, they removed the bag off my head and I saw my friend, he was the one in front of me on the floor. And then they told me to sit on the floor facing the wall. They brought another prisoner on my back and he was also naked. Then they ordered me to bend onto my knees and hands on the ground. And then they placed three others on our backs, naked. And after that they order me to sleep on my stomach and they ordered the other guy to sleep on top of me in the same position and the same way to all of us, and there were six of us. They were laughing, taking pictures, and they were stepping on our hands with their feet. And they started taking one after another and they wrote on our bodies in English. I don't know what they wrote, but they were taking pictures after that. Then, after that they forced us to walk like dogs on our hands and knees. And we had to bark like a dog and if we didn't do that, they start hitting us hard on our face and chest with no mercy. After that, they took us to our cells, took the mattresses out and dropped water on the floor and they made us sleep on our stomachs on the floor with the bags on our head and they took pictures of everything. (Hiadar Sabar Abed Miktub Al-Aboodi, 20 January, *Washington Post*, 2004)

This account collapses together a whole range of torture strategies and presents them as a seamless shopping list of events. This is the story of this torture – they did terrible things to me, one after the other, without discernible logic, apart from the logic of repetition and excess. There are some incomprehensible innovations – writing on the body that cannot be understood. There are some sexualised elements that fit the official account of breaking the spirit of Arab men by mobilising cultural taboos around sexuality. Forced nudity, being photographed nude, being forced to simulate sexual acts in front of women, being forced to simulate sexual acts with other prisoners, including friends, being placed and photographed in degrading poses with other prisoners – all of these could be regarded as exemplifying a peculiarly sexualised mode of abuse that posits sexuality as the weak point of the enemy Muslim. Of course, in other ways there is nothing innovative or peculiar about any of this testimony. Each element is familiar from previous imperial encounters, from the hooding and water torture to the animalisation of the detainees. Writing of French-occupied Algeria, Fanon reminds us that dehumanisation can become animalisation all too quickly: 'At times this Manichaeism goes to its logical conclusion and dehumanizes the native, or to speak plainly it turns him into an animal. In fact, the terms the settler uses when he mentions the native are zoological terms' (Fanon, 1967, 32).

Fanon's account of colonial torture and its impact anticipates many of the debates and tactics of the War on Terror. Marriages are corrupted by the sexual violence experienced during torture; massacres are conducted as a demonstration of the imperial might and as a warning to would-be insurgents; torturers themselves become unwell and dysfunctional, carrying violence into their domestic life (Fanon, 1967). Fanon teaches us that torture and abuse are not unfortunate anomalies, the result of a few bad apples among the occupation forces. The spectacle of occupation requires such depravities in order to assert its power. The testimony of Hiadar Sabar Abed

Miktub Al-Aboodi and others from Abu Ghraib describes a frightening, but not unfamiliar, catalogue of prison tortures. The accounts of beatings, sexual assaults, variations of shackling and water torture, could be taken from the testimonies of victims of a host of repressive regimes. The emblematic images of the War on Terror are horrible – but they are not unusual. If anything, the public focus on the pictured sexual assaults detracts from a recognition of the range, extent and institutionalisation of the abuse.

Accounts from Guantánamo provide other emblematic but, non-visual, instances of abuse. These are the glimpses of information that illuminate our understanding of the War on Terror and its uncertain battle lines. It is telling that a range of commentaries on the so-called detention facility at Guantánamo speak of black holes and other figures of the unrepresentable (Johns, 2005; Steyn, 2004; Lincoln, 2007). The use of sexual reference points is presented as an expression of contempt for Islam – our methods can make you no more than an animal, whatever your faith tells you.

> They brought pictures of naked women and dirty magazines and put them on the floor. One of the interrogators brought a cup holder for four cups with two coffees in the cup holder. He then deliberately placed the Quran on top of the coffee. He put his folder on the desk and then grabbed the Quran with his feet up on the table and read it like he was reading a magazine. He made jokes about the Quran. (Testimony of Tareq Dergoul, quoted in Human Rights Watch, 2005, 8)

The suggestion that the US and its allies have been using displays of disrespect towards Islam and desecration of the Quran as an intimidatory tactic has been repeated in a number of contexts – and has been the occasion of international protests (Watson, 2005; cageprisoners.com, 2005). The juxtaposition of pornography and sacred texts reinforces the message – what you hold sacred means nothing to us, or it represents only another means of humiliating you.

Religious belief, bodily integrity, control of your own sexuality as a precious and private thing, the ability to regulate your own bodily functions – anything that may be of personal value or a measure of dignity can be used as a focus for dehumanising abuse:

> Dergoul also said he would be chained in the interrogation room for long periods of time: 'Eventually I'd need to urinate and in the end I would try to tilt my chair and go on the floor. They were watching through a one-

way mirror. As soon as I wet myself, a woman MP would come in yelling, 'Look what you've done! You're disgusting.' (Human Rights Watch, 2005, 8)

The dubious legal advice asserting that only acts equivalent to those likely to cause organ failure, impairment or death constitute torture sought to gloss over these more elaborate and theatrical encounters, combining physical pain, stress and humiliation (Greenberg, 2006). The testimonies from Guantánamo and Abu Ghraib describe multi-faceted cultures of abuse, serial violations that move from beatings to stress to sexual assault to abuse through bodily functions, all of it punctuated by insults, shouting, bullying and threats.

> I often refused to cooperate with cell searches during prayer time. One reason was that they would abuse the Koran. Another was that the guards deliberately felt up my private parts under the guise of searching me. If I refused a cell search, MPs would call the Extreme Reaction Force [the actual name is the Initial Reaction Force] who came in riot gear with plastic shields and pepper spray. The Extreme Reaction Force entered the cell, ran in and pinned me down after spraying me with pepper spray and attacked me. The pepper spray caused me to vomit on several occasions. They poked their fingers in my eyes, banged my head on the floor and kicked and punched me and tied me up like a beast. They often forced my head into the toilet. (Testimony of Tarek Dergoul, quoted in Human Rights Watch, 2005, 21)

In this account, the ongoing threat of sexual assault is not made part of a larger narrative of supposed cultural humiliation. There are no snapshots for souvenirs. Instead this is the more familiar use of sexual violence as a reminder that the detainee has no rights, no recourse, no comeback. Sexual assault does not represent the essence or true meaning of this catalogue of abuse. It is not the 'worst' element, or the one that is designed to break the prisoner's spirit because this is the ultimate cultural humiliation, or the climax of a series of actions. It is just one more horrific assault – not more and not less than the others described. This is part of my overall argument – that sexual assault does not represent the 'meaning' of these attacks, and that to regard the sexualised element as the central component is to misunderstand the range and viciousness of these abuses. The sexual element is important not as the ultimate humiliation faced by victims, but as the comprehensible abuse relayed to international audiences. In the absence of a language to convey pain, or the sensations of prolonged stress, sleep deprivation or sensory assault, the representation of sexual abuse signals that this is torture to an audience who must be made to understand that this is being done on their behalf to protect them.

There is something like a cultural studies literature about torture – albeit a slim one – focusing on the troubled question of what can be communicated about the horror of the body in pain. This is not the extensive debate about the extent of torture, or the legal framework prohibiting torture, or the long and unhappy history of torture by all too many regimes (some of this can be seen in Levinson, 2004; Roth and Worden, 2005; Greenberg, 2006). Instead, this is a literature that examines how we can comprehend torture and, more particularly, how we can understand another person's pain (Barker, 1984; Scarry, 1985). Elaine Scarry's famous work on this issue identifies torture as a practice that makes pain visible:

> torture, which contains specific acts of inflicting pain, is also itself a demonstration and magnification of the felt-experience of pain. In the very processes it uses to produce pain within the body of the prisoner, it bestows visibility on the structure and enormity of what is usually private and incommunicable. (Scarry, 1985, 27)

Part of the horror of torture is the communication to the victim and others of what they can expect – a theatrics that seeks to display that most private of experiences, pain. The iconographic images of the War on Terror have served a similar purpose, but for a global audience. It seems that there has been a widespread knowledge within Iraq that prisoners are being abused; photographic evidence may enrage but it did not surprise Iraqis. The shock impact has been on the international public, and most of all, those from occupying nations wishing to believe, despite all previous evidence, that 'we' do not do things like that. Although I am not suggesting that the leaking of torture images forms any planned aspect of the War on Terror – I do not think that this is a case of colonial discipline gone global in order to warn the whole world that this fate awaits those who resist – I do think that the fact that it is no longer considered important to keep abuse secret is an indication of some shift in the techniques of global power. Now we are given access to images of the exercise of imperial might. There is no official record of civilian deaths in Iraq, although individual researchers and NGOs have attempted to collate reliable figures (see http://www.iraqbodycount.com), but we have all learned to recognise the symbolism of shackles and orange jumpsuits. The 'amateur' addition of the Abu Ghraib photographs becomes another warning of the power of the US-led Coalition – less an embarrassing revelation than another proof of what we can do to our enemies. In these highly theatricalised images, sexualised abuse has played a central role in condensing the meaning of torture. While neither physical pain nor the relentless horror of abuse carried out over a period of time can be captured in a static image, torture can be pictured as sexual humilia-tion, animalisation, dehumanisation. These abuses are not focused around sexual abuse above other abuses, but the representation of sexual torture makes the existence of torture comprehensible to an international audience. More than accounts of beating and other physical violence, tableaux of dehumanisation convey torture to us – and it seems to me that we are meant to know that this is going on.

Terror as secret vice

Through previous eras of covert and brutal US intervention in Latin America, activists relied on the impact of uncovering and publicising these abuses (Chomsky and Herman, 1979). If only people knew, then it couldn't happen. This belief seemed to be confirmed by the covert nature of such operations. US administrators and military com-manders regarded it as important that the general public did not know what was done in their name, and, equally importantly, were not aware of security risks triggered by previous military and intelligence operations. It was thought that the public would not accept the costs of 'blowback' – the unintended consequences of security activity, taking the form of new threats which themselves would become targets of new covert operations (Johnson, 2000). In an adaptation of the blowback argument, campaigners against torture have insisted that the use of torture is counterproductive and will become another occasion for hatred of the West and atrocities against westerners and their allies/collaborators. If we cannot be persuaded that torture is a crime against humanity, perhaps we can agree that the use of torture makes us less safe. Of course, there is some public protest against the revelations of torture by coalition troops. However, overall, there seems to be an acceptance that such things happen – not that this is right, but that this is somehow beyond our control. George

Soros suggests that when faced with the question of whether torture is acceptable if it can stop terrorist attack, people answer that they hope that this is being done without their knowledge (Soros, 2004). The War on Terror does not quite ask for our consent, but its conduct lets us know that we are implicated in horror and that there is little we can do about it.

Terror as pleasure

Perhaps this is pure evil, the unpleasant impulse to hurt because you can. In a recent discussion of the character of terror, Terry Eagleton reminds us that evil has been understood as horror with no meaning. This is cruelty as an end in itself. More than just an unhappy by-product of some ideological endeavour or political campaign, this is barbarity for the sake of fun: 'The evil are not just prepared to wade through blood, but actually relish the prospect' (Eagleton, 2005, 118). Eagleton quips that, in our time, the excessive violence occasioned by the will to absolute power is known 'for the most part as US foreign policy'. Yet he is careful to clarify that, however unpleasant they may be, members of the US administration are not evil in the sense that they unleash carnage for fun. These actions are supposed to be necessary in order to pursue some larger project – such greater goods as infinite freedom, or the battle for our way of life. And yet ... 'Even so, there is usually something in such power which is self-delighting, sadistically superfluous, maliciously excessive of its purpose' (Eagleton, 2005, 118).

The sexualised excesses of the War on Terror seem to exceed any instrumental purpose. To authorise such abuses in so open a manner seems to go against previous understandings of state security – surely it would be wise to be more discreet? Yet the various revelations of abuse carried out in the name of the War on Terror merit only the most half-hearted of denials, accompanied by warnings that such actions are necessary. If anything, these most horrible displays of power are a cause of pleasure. From Bush's laughing cowboy-isms to the grins of prison guards, this stuff is presented as fun. Slavoj Žižek has compared the manner of the photographed incidents at Abu Ghraib to the ritual initiations of US campus societies:

> The torture at Abu Ghraib was thus not simply a case of American arro-gance toward a Third World people. In being submitted to the humiliating tortures, the Iraqi prisoners were effectively *initiated into American culture*:

They got a taste of the culture's obscene underside that forms the necessary supplement to the public values of personal dignity, democracy and freedom. (Žižek, 2004)

In her insightful piece on torture, Puar expresses unease at this 'limp analogizing', because although she agrees that 'proliferating modalities of violence need and feed off one another – there is an easy disregard of the forced, nonconsensual, systemic, repetitive, and intentional order of violence hardly attributable to "rituals" that have gone "overboard"' (Puar, 2005a, 32). However, I am less sure that Žižek's analogy is trivialising. His suggestion is not that frat-boy culture is the sole or archetypal representation of American culture – rather he argues that this physical abuse represents, as he says, the necessary supplement to the public values of such a culture. To suffer such stylised abuse is to be initiated into the logic of these values – to comprehend in the most horrific of ways that this is what the occupier holds dear and, for just this reason, may take from you. The War on Terror enables a series of fairly old-style colonial occupations, but there is an additional overarching narrative that addresses the whole world. More than any previous expansionary project, the War on Terror is presented as a universal and disinterested endeavour – only the evil terrorist would wish to resist. It is this will to universalism, however fictional, that shifts the dynamic of such displays of power from the localised interaction between occupier and occupied to the global divisions of 'with us or against us'. The suggestion that there is no alternative, only the 'coalition of the willing' and an 'axis of evil' that oppresses their own populations, opens the possibility that the whole world could be initiated into American culture. However, unlike the more familiar initiations of transnational media and consumer goods, this is a threatening ritual that reminds us where the power lies and of how dangerous it would be to resist. In *Welcome to the Desert of the Real*, Žižek evokes Agamben's distinction between 'the full citizen and *Homo sacer* who, although he or she is alive as a human being, is not part of the political community' (Žižek, 2002, 91). *Homo sacer* is the being who remains alive only as an indulgence, who should be dead already – and to whom, therefore, anything can be done. Žižek ends by suggesting that the true aim of this 'war' is ourselves (154). It is we who must be made to understand the importance of these terrifying initiations.

It is an open secret that torture is employed as part of the War on Terror. In fact, this knowledge hardly qualifies as a secret at all – it is an openly acknowledged fact that is described in a manner that protects key actors from prosecution. There is no attempt to hide what is going on – only a display that lets the viewer know that culpability cannot be proven. This is the display of an absolute power that does not need to hide itself. If we express discomfort at these necessary violations, we ourselves become suspect, in need of initiation into the imperatives of this new world. For this is a 'war' that addresses the whole world, not only territories currently under occupation, and which demonstrates the costs of resistance both as a reassurance and a warning. In the process, torture must be denied, but not hidden. We are encouraged to comprehend this horror, to know that it is done in our name and that it can be done to anyone. We are supposed to feel protected, but I can't help thinking that we are also supposed to feel afraid.

Conclusion
The Spectacle of Violence

I have tried to argue throughout this book that the practices of the War on Terror are characterised by levels of sexualised intensity that go beyond anything that could be required for instrumental ends. The new imperialism clearly represents a contemporary battle for scarce resources and levers of power; however, this endeavour is supplemented by the development of newly charged myths of 'race' and sexuality. The combination of such stark material competition and emotive cultural fantasies leads to a world where the excuse of defending western interests can be used to legitimate all manner of brutality.

Ideas of gender, feminism and sexuality loom large in this machinery of expropriation and occupation. The mythologies of the War on Terror play heavily on the role of women and the need to intervene for rights and democracy to prevail. In the process, the imagined enemy of the West, the faceless extremist, becomes a highly sexualised figure. The battle ostensibly to defend western values and to propagate the culture of democracy and rights is articulated as a struggle over the correct manner in which to inhabit gender and to express sexuality. In an echo of previous imperialisms, the fear of supposedly improper gendering is harnessed as a justification for violence and exploitation. The impact on understandings of feminism and progressive gender politics is extreme and damaging and infects the conduct of international relations. Once again, the West is hated for its cultural impositions, including the apparent imposition of feminism and liberal sexual attitudes. At the same time, the conduct of western military intervention leads again to an erosion of women's rights and widespread sexual abuse. International politics continues to be cut through with mythologies of gender and sexuality, of what is proper and what is unacceptable and, once again, of safety and danger. The figure of the dangerous brown man may be no more than a half-acknowledged story, but his depiction reveals the fears and motivations of a West that is on the offensive again.

This book has argued that an analysis of the figure of the dangerous brown man, as he appears in different representations in the War on Terror, can reveal key components of contemporary western subjectivity and the deep fears that motivate the actions of western powers. Racialised mythologies embody the dark secrets of the West – and the figure of the dangerous brown man combines a reworking of longstanding sexualised racisms with such contemporary concerns as the impact of religious politics on international relations. I have argued here that the peculiar and particular excesses of the War on Terror cannot be comprehended without an analysis of the violent role of sexualised racisms. Without such an understanding, the War on Terror and its proliferating blowback across the world looks set to be a very long war indeed.

Sexual propriety and civilisational battles

In many ways the battle over the control and conduct of women is an old old story. Not much to surprise us here. There may be some new inflections to the tussle, so that team West cheers for a freedom embodied by the right to vote, romantic choice, and economic activity that enables participation in consumer markets, while the rest exalt purity, mutual respectfulness and equality and protection in the family, but the battle itself replays a familiar contest. In its contemporary incarnation, this battle is informed by feminism on both sides. The terms of the engagement are shaped by ideas of freedom and equality, and both sides proclaim their superior understanding and commitment to the rights of women. Neither tends to claim women as their property, whatever we may gather from their behaviour. However, other representations of sexuality in the War on Terror have been less predictable.

I have been trying to understand the status of War on Terror torture and rendition as an open secret. Unlike some other previous instances of western-sponsored violence and human rights violations, these events are not really hidden. Admittedly there is no open celebration of torture and illegal detention, but there is no denial that these things happen. The US may deny that it employs torture, but no one pretends that others, those such as Syria who occupy the strange status of simultaneously being allies in the War on Terror and threats along the axis of evil, do not. While Guantánamo remains all but impenetrable with even those providing legal representation to detainees rarely granted access, it also remains resolutely visible, at least in the global imagination. The US itself has released iconic images that continue to inform the global imagination – orange jumpsuits have become a global brand, recognised by all and replayed back to the West on the bodies of hapless western hostages. Torture itself may not form part of the official imagery of the War on Terror, but both the photographs from Abu Ghraib and the revelations of the torture suffered by detainees when rendered or in Guantánamo or other detention facilities have received extensive circulation with little attempt to refute the allegations. Who denies that these mutilations have taken place? If anything, we are led to believe that these unfortunate incidents occur only to those who are already subjects of suspicion, if not in fact the most evil of the evil. Torture and abuse are inexcusable of course, but how much worse are the potential crimes of these evil men?

Although these images and accounts are not designed to titillate and pleasure the audience, there is something reminiscent of pornography in the growing body of public representations of the War on Terror. Consider the available representations – mugshots of the highly significant, revealing either the depravity of desperate men or the disguise of normality that characterises the truly evil; hooded and restrained prisoners in orange boilersuits, kneeling, shackled; almost naked and carried by guards, seen through the mesh of security fencing; Abu Ghraib and all we imagine once we learn of that. In common with other representational frameworks, including that of pornography, these are images of people without social context or relations. Familiarity with the practice of consuming similar media forms conditions viewers both to accept that these people are without history or context and to extrapolate the greater horror that is implied by our glimpsed knowledge of these tableaux. We understand the enormity of the horror but are divided from the kind of understanding that explains or enables action.

The global public and offers that cannot be refused

For some time, debates about the cultural character of globalisation have suggested that the flow of information and the technology that enables instantaneous communication are both key markers of what is distinctive about our globally connected times. Much of this discussion has focused on the new possibilities of social and political engagement that such media represent. Here I want to reconsider some of these ideas as they impact on the War on Terror.

This book has argued that this endeavour combines military activity and reworkings of political relationships within nations with a cultural project to wrap people from many locations into a sense of shared participation in a global public. This global public space employs the informational cultures and technologies of globalisation. The messages of the War on Terror circulate through this diverse network of representations and information sources, and although clearly use is made of mainstream media and old-fashioned propaganda tactics, not least in the careful control of official coverage of war zones, there is also a negotiation with the more diffuse information flows of our time. This is a more knowing engagement with the cultural formations of globalised times, one that combines the urge of the powerful to control the reactions of others with an understanding that popular opinion cannot be shaped easily through didactic means any more, if ever it could. This is something like the suggestion by Aihwa Ong that the world of scapes and flows is disciplined by

> the production of transnational spaces not so much defined by flows as by the reorganization of social networks that engage state power in a variety of ways. These emerging fields of translocal connection and norm-making – in *spaces of global visibility* – are regulated by the power relations of media, trade, and financial markets. (Ong, 1997, 192)

Ong is extending and adapting an account of the cultural possibilities of a globalised world where many actors can engage actively with the production and circulation of information. Influential commentators such as Castells have argued that the globalised world represents an informational age and that the cultural codes that shape social relations are reworked through the rapid circulation of informational sources. Ong argues that the ascendance of Asian countries and the increasing influence of Asian diasporas has, 'engendered Asia-Pacific publics that not only play a role in shaping global opinions, but also in negotiating cultural power on the global stage' (Ong, 1997, 193).

In this account, Ong appeals to a concept of publicness that builds on Habermas to argue that global information flows create publics that 'participate in the production of cultural norms' (Ong, 1997, 193). For Ong, this is the world of 'media barons and tycoons', 'translocal arenas in which corporate systems compete (with each other and with state power) for control of the distribution of images, norms, and cultural knowledge across political lines' (Ong, 1997, 194).

Her interest is in non-state actors and the shaping of translocal publics, in dialogue with diasporic communities. Mine is not quite this. I am intrigued by Ong's conception of the translocal public as a space that is highly mediatised and yet is more than merely another term for transnational audiences. She summarises this thus:

> translocal publics are communicative networks that vitally re-integrate systems-world and the lifeworld *across* political boundaries. They are the arenas where the reorganization of capital, technology, and cities ('post-modernity') and the extreme commodification of culture ('post-modernism') converge in the transformation of everyday life. (Ong, 1997, 194–5)

I am interested in this idea of a translocal public that can shape norms and cultural knowledge. This is an important acknowledge-ment of the place of media and information flows in the construction of public consciousness in globally integrated arenas. Recent history shows that state machineries now compete with global information flows to shape public understandings of events and state actions. Human rights activists, international institutions and interventionary states all rely on this flow of information in their attempts to construct global standards of state conduct, and I do not wish to suggest that these various illicit, independent or non-official sources bring no benefit to public cultures. However, I do want to argue that we should reconsider the excessive optimism of earlier accounts of new media forms and circuits. Whereas the possibility of democratised media use remains a motivation and aspiration for many participants, states and other powerful agents have understood that intervention in this global public realm is an essential component of wielding global influence. Equally, non-state actors have become engaged in the global public through internet broadcasting and distribution of digital images.

In our time, what can be seen and known through this formation becomes an oblique commentary on where power lies – a development of state power within national boundaries and an attempt to intervene in a global sphere in a manner that reconstructs that power in transnational form. This assertion of power operates through a variety of means. There are familiar examples of state propaganda and the dissemination of official information. Some journalists are embedded with advancing military forces. Others are ushered around carefully policed tours of illegal detention facilities. Allegations of evildoing are broadcast about people who have no opportunity to refute such slurs. At the same time other forms of information are blocked – who is detained and where? How are War on Terror prisoners transported around the world, on which planes, landing on which airstrips? Alongside all of this information management, there is another aspect to the circulation of knowledge in the War on Terror. Although many aspects of the War on Terror are presented as secrets necessary for security purposes, key elements of these supposed secrets are widely known although rarely acknowledged in official discourses. Many details of the process and excesses of extraordinary rendition are known, from a variety of sources, and these fragments circulate to create a certain kind of public knowledge of what rendition means. Although the internal workings of Guantánamo may be presented as top secret, a whole series of suggestions about what happens there have entered the information flows of the War on Terror. Most of the iconic images and stories that together create the sense of public knowledge of the workings of the War on Terror cannot easily be traced to a single source. Instead, the fragments work together to convey a knowledge that terrible things are being done in the name of 'our' values and way of life, while obscuring the lines of responsibility for such actions. These are knowledges that are not denied by official sources, but which, equally, are not acknowledged. Therefore we know that Maher Arar was held in a coffin-sized cell, that Khaled el-Masri was abducted, held and released in secret, that Binyam Mohammad has been tortured with razor blades, that Omar Deghayes has lost an eye in the course of his illegal imprisonment. We know that hundreds of men and boys have been detained at Guantánamo and that we will never know most of their names. We know that hundreds more are held in secret prisons across the world, that torture is carried out in our name in these secret locations, that prisoners die at the hands of interrogators who claim to be defending our way of life. These knowledges function as substantial rumours, never quite verifiable, but endlessly contagious.

Of course, much of what we know is the result of tireless work by human rights activists and lawyers, and every snippet of information has been battled over before it enters the catalogue of popular knowledge. However, despite the heavy-handed attempts to control such information, in another sense none of this has been strictly secret. The purpose and nature of Guantánamo were proclaimed openly from the first transportation of prisoners. The statements of US and, occasionally, UK officials have affirmed the necessity of extreme measures, while never quite admitting to any particular allegation.

The War on Terror attempts to create a transnational coalition of nations that can combine to initiate military interventions without recourse to previously understood limitations of international law, instead operating as an alternative international community that is not bound by formal decision making but which itself operates as a cultural tendency. Alongside this explicitly military function, the Coalition operates to normalise anti-terrorism tactics within national spaces. Entry into this club of mutual reinforcement and support requires co-operation in key aspects of security activity. Most controversially, the War on Terror has resurrected a transnational torture and detention network, and unlike earlier incarnations of this dubious co-operation, has made the existence of this horror an open secret. The existence of illegal prisons, extraordinary rendition and torture has become a well-known aspect of this long war – not denied, but instead not admitted but justified with reference to our newly dangerous times.

It is this accumulation of horror that is not secret that leads me to argue that circulating knowledge of abuse acts as a decisive inter-vention in the space of the global public. This is not a dangerous secret to be exposed but serves as an active component of how the global public is constructed by powerful nations in contestation with so-called enemies of the West. The unwilling audience to these acts becomes anchored into the terms of the War on Terror through the knowing manner in which Coalition and other powers allow fragments of information that can inhabit a mediatised framework of spectatorship and empathy.

The exercise of power also has learned from these years of media and information saturation (Thrift, 2005), and the call to suitably disciplined subjects of this transglobal constellation of power comes through the expert use of informational means. What we see and know and how we feel about it become central to our construction as functioning citizen-viewers of the global public. Understanding and participating in these messages is one marker of what it is to be accepted as human in our time. The barbarians are those beyond this contract of circulating knowledges. I have argued that, in our time, the spectre of sexuality fulfils a number of important functions in this display.

Lilie Chouliaraki has a more optimistic view of the development of global media audiences, but she, too, understands television (and by implication other transnational media forms) as a technique of governance:

> at the moment when CNN or the BBC addresses the spectator as a global citizen of the 'be the first to know' or 'putting news first' type that their news broadcasts also reproduce a certain version of world order, defined by space-times of safety and danger and hierarchies of human life. In this sense, mediation as a governmental technology is neither purely regulatory nor purely benign. (Chouliaraki, 2006, 61)

This is something like the space of the global public that I am seeking. This interpellation of the global audience is hailed via transnational media forms and it both positions us and opens new possibilities of interpretation. For Chouliaraki, despite the governmental intervention, possibility outweighs regulation. She presents this space as an embryonic possibility of a cosmopolitan citizenship based on ethical engagement across borders: 'The spectators are now members of a world bigger than just the West, who develop their self-identity and disposition to act on this world in response to visions of the public that television itself proposes' (Chouliaraki, 2006, 190). My fear is that the response that is elicited is a kind of knowing helplessness, horror mixed with an acceptance that, of course, this is how great powers will behave. As Jacques Bricmont suggests, who really expected anything other than this sadism combined with idiocy, racism combined with ignorance, all wrapped in a covering of pretended cultural understanding (Bricmont, 2006). This is what great military powers do when subduing weak enemies, and those who live under their protection cannot pretend that they do not know this.

The slogan of the anti-war movement protesting against US-led attacks on Afghanistan and Iraq has been 'Not in Our Name'. The claim is that without our consent these 'defences of democracy' cannot be legitimate, and also that the actions of our governments are not authorised by us. The slogan also alludes more obliquely to the shifting structure of feeling that I have tried to outline here, and articulates a refusal of the emotional blackmail of the government claim that these horrors are carried out for us, with regret but as a necessary defence of our way of life.

However, although I understand and support the sentiments of the slogan, I also fear that refusal is not so easy. The claim by states that horrific actions have been carried out in the name of their populations, in the interests of defending the privileges of those populations, forms one central component in the construction of a global public. It is a move that takes place alongside a range of other claims and techniques that seek to create a different relation between state, citizen and global action. I do not dispute that many many people continue to resist these processes and protest against the actions of their own and other governments; however I do not think that stating our refusal to co-operate or to recognise the legitimacy of such actions extracts us from the suffocating disciplinary network of this new machinery of government. Some elements of the position of global audience come into play even as the protest is articulated, which is not to say that protest is futile or ineffective, but to argue that the War on Terror has, in fact, altered the dynamic and framework of political life and, for many parts of the world, has shifted the relation between state and citizen in important ways.

My contention has been that within these shifts that engulf us all, whether or not we consent to the militarised aggression being conducted in our name, mythologies of race and sexuality serve as carriers for some important cultural work. We have seen that the War on Terror mobilises a range of racialised tropes, while not being easily reduced to a war about racism, and that the pursuit of this war refers to many sexualised images and ideas while having little to say directly about sex.

The construction of a global public as audience to the War on Terror and as a particular relation to the situations of witnessing and being governed operates through a series of positionings. Overall, the construction as audience is framed to implicate the viewer in the supposedly necessary horrors of counterterrorism.

At the same time, the representations of both our way of life and the 'horrific but necessary' abuses suffered by terrorist suspects reference ideals of sexual freedom and autonomy, because these ideals have held a special status in how western cultures depict freedom. Both the images and rumours of torture and abuse render audiences guilty and complicit in a highly knowing version of the pornographic gaze. Here our displeasure counts for nothing because the fact of our witness completes the pornographic tableau.

The horror that is displayed to willing and unwilling audiences takes its sense from hegemonic and shared ideas of pleasure and freedom. This is the concept that Gail Hawkes identifies as the place of sex and pleasure in western culture, a process that builds on Christian notions of bodily discipline and surveillance cultures that conjure identities from acts to develop a blending of consumer and sexual pleasures in the promotion of freedom as a right to sexual entertainment.

At the same time as all of this, there are violent manifestations of gender anxiety in many parts of the world. The turbulence of contemporary global events, whether in terms of the increasing precariousness of basic survival for many, the terrible eruptions of armed conflict within and between nations, the continuing and sometimes escalating levels of violent repression by authoritarian regimes of various inclinations, or the everyday rapacity of capital and the (non-news of) war on the poor, has impacts on all these levels on gendering and sexuality. In many instances, women and girls are made scapegoats for the unhappy changes flooding through ordinary lives – and the disciplinary revenge tactics of past centuries reappear in rape epidemics in South Africa and Mexico and the re-emergence, after years of significant progress and public participation for women, of so-called traditional practices of honour killing in Pakistan, Palestine and Iraq.

The suggestion that gender imbalance and/or restriction of access to women for young men can become a cause of dangerous social pressure has entered serious scholarship (Hudson and Den Boer, 2004). Both China and India face a coming generation that is short of women – with both states concerned that this may create a substantial grouping of non-attached men who neither benefit from the stabilising influence of regular heterosexual sex or have the social investments that come from the ties of affective and familial relations. Such accounts are not so far from the speculation about the roots of Islamic radicalisation and terror. These parallel discussions point to the pressure point of unfulfilled young men, unable to marry or form relationships as a result of strict cultural codes and a lack of economic opportunities. Submerged in all of these accounts is a presumption that women serve as an outlet for male sexual urges and that without access to this pacifying outlet, male sexual energy is likely to burst out as violence in some other arena.

If the goal of humanitarian intervention has become to convince dangerous brown men all over the world that there are benefits to participation in liberal democracy, commodity culture and women's rights, then these benefits continue to be coded through the objectification of women's bodies. At the same time, perceived threats to the West are countered through strategies of repression enabled by mythologies of sexualised racism, a set of myths that serves both to demonise the other and to corral insiders into collusion with powerful protectors. Who can refuse the values of equality, human rights, freedom and the right freely to form affective relations as a mark of our deepest humanity? We know as we witness the horror carried out in our name that this war debases these values, but our witness is characterised by bad faith, for to defend the truth of such values must imply that this is in essence a good war, if only it could be returned to its central values. The rulers of the world do not seek to soften this dilemma or to hide it from us – our discomfort places us in the global public as properly disciplined subjects of new processes of governance quite as effectively as gung-ho obedience. Writing of another, earlier time (which to nostalgic eyes now seems so innocent), Peter Sloterdijk describes a similar unhappy consciousness that displaces ideological critique and the belief that knowing can bring enlightenment. This is cynical reason that knows of the ways of the world but accepts that nothing else is possible.

> To act against better knowledge is today the global situation in the superstructure; it knows itself to be without illusions and yet to have been dragged down by the 'power of things'. Thus what is regarded in logic as a paradox and in literature as a joke appears in reality as the actual state of affairs. (Sloterdijk, 1988, 6)

References

Abbas, Tahir (2007) *Islamic Political Radicalism: A European Perspective,* Edinburgh, Edinburgh University Press

ABC News (2006) 'Suicide Bombers' Mother Elected to Palestinian Parliament', http://abcnews.go.com/International/ print?id=1536576, 24/1/06

ABC News Online (2005) 'CIA Renditions Began under Clinton: Agent', www.abc.net.au, 29/12/05

Abramsky, Sasha (2007) 'From White House to Abu Ghraib', www.guardian.co.uk/ commentisfree , 26/4/07

Abu Khalil, As'ad (2001) 'Sex and the Suicide Bomber', http://dir.salon.com, 7/11/01

Ackerly, Brooke A.; Stern, Maria; True, Jacqui (2006) *Feminist Methodologies for International Relations*, Cambridge, Cambridge University Press

ACLU (2005) 'Extraordinary Rendition – Fact Sheet', New York, American Civil Liberties Union, 12/6/2005

Adams, Mary Louise (1997) *The Trouble with Normal: Postwar Youth and the Making of Heterosexuality*, Toronto, University of Toronto

Adkins, Lisa (1995) *Gendered Work, Sexuality, Family and the Labour Market*, Buckingham, Open University Press

Aitken, Robert (2008) *An Investigation into Cases of Deliberate Abuse and Unlawful Killing in Iraq in 2003 and 2004* (the Aitken Report), London, Ministry of Defence

Al-Ali, Nadje (2005) 'Reconstructing Gender: Iraqi Women between Dictatorship, War, Sanctions and Occupation', *Third World Quarterly*, Vol. 26, Nos 4–5

Albanese, Patrizia (2006) *Mothers of the Nation: Women, Families and Nationalism in Twentieth Century Europe*, Toronto, University of Toronto Press

Alexander, Elizabeth (1994) ' "Can you be BLACK and look at this?": Reading the Rodney King Video(s)', in Thelma Golden (ed.), *Black Male, Representations of Masculinity in Contemporary American Art*, New York, Whitney Museum of American Art

Alexander, M. Jacqui (1996) *Feminist Genealogies, Colonial Legacies, Democratic Futures*, New York, Routledge

Alexander, M. Jacqui (2005) *Pedagogies of Crossing: Meditations on Feminism, Sexual Politics, Memory and the Sacred*, Durham, Duke University Press

Al-Hassan Golley, Nawar (2004) 'Is Feminism Relevant to Arab Women?' *Third World Quarterly*, Vol. 25, No. 3

Ali, Suki (2000) 'Introduction: Trying to Connect You', in Suki Ali, Kelly Coate and Wangui Wa Goro, *Global Feminist Politics, Identities in a Changing World*, London, Routledge

145

Alibhai-Brown, Yasmin (2000) *After Multiculturalism*, London, Foreign Policy Centre

Allen, Beverly (1996) *Rape Warfare: Hidden Genocide in Bosnia-Herzegovina and Croatia*, Minneapolis, University of Minnesota Press

Allen, James; Lewis, Jon; Litwack, Leon F. (2000) *Without Sanctuary: Photographs and Postcards of Lynching in America*, Santa Fe, New Mexico, Twin Palms

Allin, Dana H.; Andreani, Gilles; Errera, Phillippe; Gary, Samore (2007) *Repairing the Damage: Possibilities and Limits of Transatlantic Consensus*, London, Routledge

Allison, Rebecca (2004) 'Student in US Jail after Airport Bomb Joke', *Guardian* 21/1/04

Alloula, Malek (1986) *The Colonial Harem*, Minneapolis, University of Minnesota Press

AlSayyad, Nelar; Castells, Manuel (2002) *Muslim Europe or Euro-Islam: Politics, Culture and Citizenship in the Age of Globalization*, Lanham MD, Lexington Books

Amin, Samir (2004) *The Liberal Virus, Permanent War and the Americanization of the World*, London, Pluto

Amis, Martin (2006) 'The Age of Horrorism', *Observer*, 10/9/06

Amis, Martin (2007) *The Second Plane: September 11, 2001–2007*, London, Jonathan Cape

Amnesty International (2004) *It's In Our Hands: Stop Violence Against Women*, Oxford, Alden Press

Amnesty International (2005) 'Iraq: Decades of Suffering, Now Women Deserve Better', London, Amnesty International, AI Index MDE14/001/2005

Amnesty International (2007) Egypt – Systematic Abuses in the Name of Security, Amnesty International, AI Index, MDE 12/001/2007

Anderson, David (2005) *Histories of the Hanged: Britain's Dirty War in Kenya and the End of Empire*, London, Weidenfeld

Ankersen, Christopher (2007) *Understanding Global Terror*, Cambridge, Polity

Arcel, L.T. (1998) 'Sexual Torture of Women as a Weapon of War – The Case of Bosnia-Herzegovina', *European Psychiatry*, Vol.13, Supp. 4

Archer, John E. (2000) *Social Unrest and Popular Protest in England, 1780–1840*, Cambridge, Cambridge University Press

Archer, Louise (2001) '"Muslim Brothers, Black Lads, Traditional Asians": British Muslim Young Men's Constructions of Race, Religion and Masculinity', *Feminism and Psychology*, Vol. 11, No. 1

Armour, Rollin, Sr (2002), *Islam, Christianity and the West: A Troubled History*, Maryknoll, NY: Orbis

Armstrong, Karen (1994) *A History of God: The 4000 Year Quest of Judaism, Christianity and Islam*, New York, Ballantine Books

Atasoy, Yildiz (2006) 'Governing Women's Morality: A Study of Islamic Veiling in Canada', *European Journal of Cultural Studies*, 9

Ayotte, Kevin J.; Husain, Mary (2005) 'Securing Afghan Women: Neocolonialism, Epistemic Violence, and the Rhetoric of the Veil', *NWSA Journal*, Vol. 17, No. 3

Bacchetta, Paola; Campt, Tina; Grewal, Inderpal; Kaplan, Caren; Moallem, Minoo; Terry, Jennifer (2001) 'Transnational Feminist Practices against War', October 2001, www.geocities.com/carenkaplan03/transnationalstatement.html

Back, Les (2007) *The Art of Listening*, Oxford, Berg

Baker, Peter (2006) 'Bush tells group he sees a "third awakening"', *Washington Post*, 13/9/06

Banks, Christopher (2004) 'Protecting (or Destroying) Freedom through Law: The USA PATRIOT Act's Constitutional Implications' in David B. Cohen and John W. Wells (eds), *American National Security and Civil Liberties in an Era of Terrorism*, Basingstoke, Palgrave Macmillan.

Barker, Francis (1984) *The Tremulous Private Body*, London, Methuen

Bashi, Vina (2004) 'Globalized anti-blackness: Transnationalizing Western Immigration Law, Policy, and Practice', *Ethnic and Racial Studies* Vol. 27, No. 4, July 2004

BBC News (2005) 'Afghan Women "Still Suffer"', http://news.bbc.co.uk/2/hi/south_asia/4592697.stm

BBC News (2007) 'Blair Feared Faith "Nutter" Label', http://news.bbc.co.uk, 25/11/07

Beattie, Tina (2007) 'Religion in the Blair Era', www.opendemocracy.net, 10/1/07

Begg, Moazzam (2006) *Enemy Combatant: A British Muslim's Journey to Guantánamo and Back*, London, Free Press

Bellamy, Alex J. (2006) 'No Pain, No Gain? Torture and Ethics in the War on Terror' *International Affairs* Vol. 82, No. 1

Bergsten, C. Fred (1990) 'The World Economy after the Cold War', *Foreign Affairs*, Summer 1990

Better, Shirley Jean (2002) *Institutional Racism: A Primer on Theories and Strategies for Social Change*, Lanham MD, Rowman & Littlefield

'Beyond "Feminism Versus Multiculturalism": Revisiting the relationship between power, beliefs, identity and values', School of Law, King's College London, LSE Gender Institute and AHRC Research Centre for Law, Gender and Sexuality, London School of Economics, 17 November 2006. http://www.kent.ac.uk/clgs/documents/Feminism_Multicult_Report_final.pdf

Bhatt, Chetan (1997) *Liberation and Purity: Race, New Religious Movements and the Ethics of Postmodernity*, London, UCL Press

Bhatt, Chetan (2001) *Hindu Nationalism: Origins, Ideologies and Modern Myths*, Oxford, Berg

Bhattacharyya, Gargi (1998) *Tales of Dark-Skinned Women*, London, UCL Press

Bhattacharyya, Gargi (2008) 'Globalizing Racism and Myths of the Other in the War on Terror', in Lentin 2008

Bhattacharyya, G.; Gabriel, J.; Small, S. (2001) *Race and Power*, London, Routledge

Bhavnani, Reena; Mirza, Heidi Safia; Meetoo, Veena (2005) *Tackling the Roots of Racism: Lessons for Success*, London, Policy Press

Blair, Tony (2006) 'The Duty to Integrate: Shared British Values', www.pmo.gov.uk, 8/12/06

Blakeley, Ruth (2007) 'Why Torture?', *Review of International Studies*, Vol. 33, No. 3

Blond, Phillip; Pabst, Adrian (2006) 'The Twisted Religion of Blair and Bush', *International Herald Tribune*, 10/3/06

Booth, Ken; Dunne, Tim (2002) *Worlds in Collision, Terror and the Future of Global Order*, Houndmills, Basingstoke, Palgrave Macmillan

Bordo, Susan (1999) *The Male Body: A New Look at Men in Public and in Private*, New York, Farrar, Strauss & Giroux

Bourke, J. (1999) *An Intimate History of Killing: Face to Face Killing in Twentieth Century Warfare*, New York, Basic Books

Bowker, David W. (2006) 'Unwise Counsel', in Karen J. Greenberg, *The Torture Debate in America*, Cambridge, Cambridge University Press

Bowling, Ben (1998) *Violent Racism: Victimisation, Policing and Social Control*, Oxford, Oxford University Press

Bowling, Ben (2004) *Policing, Race and Racism*, Uffculme, Devon, Willan Publishing

Boyarin, Daniel (1997) *Unheroic Conduct: The Rise of Heterosexuality and the Invention of the Jewish Man*, Berkeley, University of California Press

Boyarin, Jonathan (1996) *Thinking in Jewish*, Chicago, University of Chicago Press

Boyle, Kevin (2004) 'Terrorism, States of Emergency and Human Rights' in Yotopoulos and Benedek 2004

Branigan, Tania; Cowan, Rosie (2004) 'Freed Briton tells of beatings', *Guardian*, 12/3/04

Bricmont, Jean (2006) *Humanitarian Imperialism, Using Human Rights to Sell War*, New York, Monthly Review Press

Bright, Martin (2006) 'Rendition: the cover-up', *New Statesman*, London, 23/01/06

Brittain, Victoria (2006) 'Guantánamo: A Feminist Perspective on US Human Rights Violations', *Meridians: Feminism, Race, Transnationalism*, Vol. 6, No. 2

Brodsky, Anne E. (2003) *With All Our Strength: The Revolutionary Association of the Women of Afghanistan*, New York and London, Routledge

Brown, Gordon (2007) Speech to Commonwealth Club, www.guardian.co.uk, 27/2/07

Brownmiller, Susan (1993) *Against Our Will: Men, Women and Rape*, New York, Fawcett Columbine

Bruck, Gabriele vom (2008) 'Naturalising, Neutralising Women's Bodies: The "Headscarf Affair" and the Politics of Representation', *Identities*, Vol. 15, No. 1

Bufacchi, Vittorio; Arrigo, Jean Maria (2006) 'Torture, Terrorism and the State: A Refutation of the Ticking-Bomb Argument', *Journal of Applied Philosophy*, Vol. 23, No. 3

Bulbeck, Chilla (1997) *Re-orienting Western Feminism*, Cambridge, Cambridge University Press

Burkeman, Oliver; Borger, Julian (2003) 'War critics astonished as US hawk admits invasion was illegal', *Guardian*, 20/11/03

Burton, Antoinette (1994) *Burdens of History*, Chapel Hill, University of North Carolina Press

Buruma, Ian; Margalit, Avishai (2004) *Occidentalism: The West in the Eyes of its Enemies*, London, Penguin

Bush, George (2001) 'President Discusses War on Terrorism in Address to the Nation', World Congress Center, 2001

Bush, George (2004) 'President Bush Reaffirms Resolve to War on Terror, Iraq and Afghanistan', Remarks by the President on Operation Iraqi Freedom and Operation Enduring Freedom, The East Room, http://www.whitehouse.gov/news/releases/2004/03/20040319-3.html, 19/3/2004

Bush, George (2008) BBC interview in full, http://news.bbc.co.uk/1/hi/world/americas/7245670.stm

Bush, Laura (2001) Radio address to the nation, 17 November 2001

cageprisoners.com (2005) 'Report into the systematic and institutionalised US desecration of the Qur'an and other Islamic rituals, Testimonies from former Guantánamo Bay detainees', May 2005, www.cageprisoners.com

Califia, Pat (1994) *Public Sex: The Culture of Radical Sex*, Pittsburgh and San Francisco, Cleis Press

CAMPACC (2004) 'The end of internment? The Law Lords' ruling on indefinite detention', Campaign against Criminalising Communities, www.campacc.org.uk, 23/12/04

Carby, Hazel (2000) Race Men, Harvard, Harvard University Press

Carby, Hazel (2004) 'A strange and bitter crop: the spectacle of torture', www.open-democracy.net, 11/10/04

Carr, Matt (2006) 'You are Now Entering Eurabia', *Race and Class*, Vol. 48, No. 1

Chakrabarti, Shami; Crossman, Gareth (2007) 'The First Victim of War: Compromising Civil Liberties', *Britian and Security*, http://www.liberty-human-rights.org.uk/publications/pdfs/the-first-victim-of-war-smith-institute.pdf

Chandler, David (2006) From Kosovo to Kabul and Beyond, Human Rights and International Intervention, London, Pluto

Chang, Iris (1998) The Rape of Nanking: The Forgotten Holocaust of World War II, London, Penguin

Chaudhuri, N.; Strobel, M. (1990) *Western Women and Imperialism*, Oxford, Pergamon Press

Cheyette, Bryan (1996) *Between 'Race' and Culture: Representations of 'The Jew' in English and American Literature*, Palo Alto, Stanford University Press

Chomsky, Noam; Herman, Edward S. (1979) *The Washington Connection and Third World Fascism, The Political Economy of Human Rights: Volume 1*, Boston, South End Press

Choongh, Satnam (1997) *Policing as Social Discipline*, Oxford, Clarendon Press

Choudhury, Barnie (2001) 'My allegiance is to Allah', news.bbc.co.uk, 29/10/01

Choudhury, Tufyal (2007) 'The Role of Muslim Identity Politics in Radicalisation (A Study in Progress)', Department of Communities and Local Government, http://www.communities.gov.uk

Chouliaraki, Lilie (2006) *The Spectatorship of Suffering*, London, Sage

Chowdhry, Geeta; Nair, Sheila (2004) *Power, Postcolonialism and International Relations*, New York, Routledge

Chowdhury, Subrata Roy (1989) *Rule of Law in a State of Emergency: The Paris Minimum Standards of Human Rights Norms in a State of Emergency*, New York, Pinter

Christian, Diane (2005) 'Ritual and Sexual Torture in Gitmo and Abu Ghraib, Bad Blood', www.counterpunch.org, 24/2/05

Chua, Amy (2003) *World on Fire: How Exporting Free Market Democracy Breeds Ethnic Hatred and Global Instability*, London, William Heinemann

Clegg, Jenny (1994) *Fu Manchu and the 'Yellow Peril'*, Stoke-on-Trent, Trentham

Cloud, Dana (2004) 'To Veil the Threat of Terror', *Quarterly Journal of Speech*, Vol. 9, No. 3

Cockburn, Cynthia (2007) *From Where We Stand: War, Women's Activism and Feminist Analysis*, London, Zed

Cohen, Irwin M.; Corrado, Raymond R. (2005) 'State Torture in the Contemporary World', *International Journal of Comparative Sociology* Vol. 46, No. 1–2

Cohen, Nick (2007) *What's Left? How Liberals Lost Their Way*, London, Fourth Estate

Collins, Patricia Hill (1995) *Black Feminist Thought: Knowledge, Consciousness, and the Politics of Empowerment*, Boston: Unwin Hyman.

Collins, Patricia Hill (2005) *Black Sexual Politics: African Americans, Gender and the New Racism*, New York, Routledge

Colls, Rachel (2004) '"Looking Alright, Feeling Alright": Emotions, Sizing and the Geographies of Women's Experiences of Clothing Consumption', *Social and Cultural Geography*, Vol. 5, No. 4

Cooper, Davina (1995) *Power in Struggle: Feminism, Sexuality and the State*, New York, New York University Press

Cooper, Robert (2004) *The Breaking of Nations: Order and Chaos in the Twenty-First Century*, London, Grove

Coote, Anna (2000) *New Gender Agenda*, London, IPPR

Croft, S. (2006) *Culture, Crisis and America's War on Terror*, Cambridge, Cambridge University Press

Daase, Christopher; Kessler, Oliver (2007) 'Knowns and Unknowns in the "War on Terror": Uncertainty and the Political Construction of Danger', *Security Dialogue*, Vol. 38: 411

Danner, M. (2004) 'Torture and Truth', in M. Danner, *Abu Ghraib: The Politics of Torture*, Berkeley, North Atlantic Books

Darby, Robert (2003) 'The Masturbation Taboo and the Rise of Routine Male Circumcision: A Review of the Historiography', *Journal of Social History*, Spring 2003

Daulatzai, Sohail (2007) 'Protect ya neck: Muslims and the Carceral Imagination in the Age of Guantánamo', *Souls: A Critical Journal of Black Politics, Culture and Society*, Vol. 9, Issue 2, April–June

Dauphinee, Elizabeth (2007) 'The Politics of the Body in Pain: Reading the Ethics of Imagery', *Security Dialogue*, Vol. 38, No. 2, June

Davis, Angela (1999) *The Prison Industrial Complex*, CD-Rom (audiobook), Oakland, CA, AK Press

Davis, Angela Y. (2003) *Are Prisons Obsolete?* New York, Seven Stories Press

De Mel, Neloufer (2001) *Women and the Nation's Narrative: Gender and Nationalism in Twentieth Century Sri Lanka*, London, Rowman & Littlefield

DelPlato, Joan (2002) *Multiple Wives, Multiple Pleasures: Representing the Harem 1800–1875*, Madison NJ, Fairleigh Dickinson University Press

deMause, Lloyd (2002) *The Emotional Life of Nations*, New York, Karnac Books, http://www.psychohistory.com

Dent, Gina (1992) *Black Popular Culture*, Seattle, Bay Press

Dershowitz, Alan (2002) 'Want to Torture? Get a Warrant', *San Francisco Chronicle*, 22 January 2002

Dillon, Sam (1991) *Comandos: The CIA and Nicaragua's Contra Rebels*, New York, Henry Holt

Dodd, Vikram (2004) 'Torture by the book', *Guardian*, 6/4/04

Dorfman, Ariel (2004) 'The Tyranny of Terror: Is Torture Inevitable in Our Century and Beyond?', in Levinson 2004

Douglass, Frederick (1982) *Narrative of the Life of Frederick Douglass, American Slave 1845*, edited and with an introduction by Houston A. Baker Jr., New York, Penguin

Dow, Mark (2005) *American Gulag: Inside US Immigration Prisons*, Berkeley and LA, University of California Press

Doy, Gen (2000) *Black Visual Culture, Modernity and Postmodernity*, London, I.B. Tauris

Drury, Shadia B. (2006) *Terror and Civilisation: Christianity, Politics and the Western Psyche*, New York, Palgrave Macmillan

Dubensky, Joyce S.; Lavery, Rachel (2006) 'Torture: An Interreligious Debate', in Karen J. Greenberg (ed.), *The Torture Debate in America*, Cambridge, Cambridge University Press

Duffield, M. (2001) *Global Governance and the New Wars: The Merging of Development and Security*, London, Zed

Durham, Martin (1998) *Fascism and Women*, London, Routledge

Eagleton, Terry (2005) *Holy Terror*, Oxford, Oxford University Press

Eisenstein, Zillah (2004) *Against Empire: Feminisms, Racism and the West*, London, Zed

Eisenstein, Zillah (2006) 'Is "W" for Women?', in Krista Hunt and Kim Rygiel (eds), *(En)Gendering the War on Terror: War Stories and Camouflaged Politics*, Aldershot, Ashgate

Eisenstein, Zillah (2007) *Sexual Decoys: Gender, Race and War in Imperial Democracy*, London, Zed

Ekklesia (2008) 'Evangelical leader's stance makes him unfit for equality post, say gay Christians', www.ekklesia.co.uk, 22/1/08

Elkins, Caroline (2005) *Britain's Gulag: The Brutal End of Empire in Kenya*, London, Cape

Ellison, Graham; Smyth, Jim (2000) *The Crowned Harp: Policing Northern Ireland*, London, Pluto

Emory Tolnay, Stewart; Beck, E. M. (1995) *A Festival of Violence: An Analysis of the Lynching of African-Americans in the American South, 1882–1930*, University of Illinois Press

English, Robert; Halperin, Jonathan (1987) *The Other Side: How Soviets and Americans Perceive Each Other*, New Brunswick, Transaction Press

Enloe, Cynthia (1983) *Does Khaki become you? The Militarisation of Women's Lives*, London, Pluto

Enloe, Cynthia (1993) *The Morning After: Sexual Politics at the End of the Cold War*, Berkeley, University of California Press

Enloe, Cynthia (2000) *Maneuvers: The International Politics of Militarizing Women's Lives*, Berkeley, University of California Press

Enloe, Cynthia (2004) *The Curious Feminist: Searching for Women in a New Age of Empire*, Berkeley, University of California Press

Enloe, Cynthia (2007) 'Feminist Readings on Abu Ghraib: Introduction', *International Feminist Journal of Politics*, 9:1

Esposito, John L. (2002) *Unholy War: Terror in the Name of Islam*, Oxford, Oxford University Press

Etzioni, Amitai (2006) 'The Global Importance of Illiberal Moderates', *Cambridge Review of International Affairs*, 19:3

European Union (2004) *Handbook on Concepts and Methods for Mainstreaming Gender Equality*, Brussels, EU

Fanon, Franz (1967) *The Wretched of the Earth*, Harmondsworth, Penguin

Fausto-Sterling, Anne (1999) *Sexing the Body: Gender Politics and the Construction of Sexuality*, New York, Basic Books

Fekete, Liz (2001) 'The Emergence of Xeno-Racism', *Race and Class*, Vol. 43, No. 2

Fekete, Liz (2006) 'Enlightened Fundamentalism? Immigration, Feminism and the Right', *Race and Class*, Vol. 48, No. 1

Fekete, Liz (2007) 'Detained: Foreign Children in Europe', *Race and Class*, Vol. 49, No. 1

Feldman, Allen (2004) 'Abu Ghraib: ceremonies of nostalgia', www.opendemocracy.net, 18/10/04

Felsenstein, Frank (1995) *Anti-Semitic Stereotypes: A Paradigm of Otherness in English Popular Culture, Baltimore,* Johns Hopkins University Press

Ferguson, Moira (1987) *The History of Mary Prince, A West Indian Slave, Related by Herself,* 1831, London, Pandora

Fetzer, Joel S. (2000) 'Economic Self-interest or Cultural Marginality? Anti-immigrant Sentiment in Nativist Political Movements in France, Germany and the USA', *Journal of Ethnic and Migration Studies*, Vol. 26, No, 1

Fletcher, George P. (2004) 'Black Hole in Guantánamo Bay', *Journal of International Criminal Justice*, Vol. 2, No. 1

Foley, Brian J. (2004) 'A nation without a conscience: why the outrage about Abu Ghraib?', May 2004, www.counterpunch.org

Foot, Rosemary (2006) 'Torture: the Struggle over a Peremptory Norm in a Counter-terrorist Era', *International Relations*, Vol. 20

Foreign and Commonwealth Office Gender Advisory Group (2004) *Inclusive Government: Mainstreaming Gender Equality in Foreign Policy*, London, Foreign and Commonwealth Office

Fox, Marie; Thomson, Michael (2005) 'Short Changed? The Law and Ethics of Male Circumcision', *International Journal of Children's Rights*, Vol. 13

Frost, Robin (2005) 'Terrorist Psychology, Motivation and Strategy', *Adelphi Papers*, Vol. 45, No. 378

Fuss, Diana (1990) *Essentially Speaking: Feminism, Nature and Difference*, London, Routledge

Gallala, Imen (2006) 'The Islamic Headscarf: An Example of Surmountable Conflict between Shari'a and the Fundamental Principles of Europe', *European Law Journal*, Vol. 12, No. 5

Garrett, Paul Michael (2007) 'Sinbin solutions: the "pioneer" projects for "problem families" and the forgetfulness of social policy research', *Critical Social Policy*, Vol. 27, No. 2

Giddens, A. (1998) *The Third Way: Renewal of Social Democracy*, Cambridge, Polity

Gillan, Audrey; Yafai, Faisal Al (2005) 'Control Order Flaws Exposed', *Guardian*, 24/3/05

Gillespie, Marie (2006) 'Security, Media, Legitimacy: Multi-Ethnic Media Publics and the Iraq War 2003', *International Relations,* Vol. 20

Gillespie, Marie (2007) 'Security, Media and Multicultural Citizenship: A Collaborative Ethnography', *European Journal of Cultural Studies*, Vol. 10

Gilman, Sander (1985) *Difference and Pathology: Stereotypes of Sexuality, Race, and Madness*, Ithaca, Cornell University Press

Gilman, Sander (1991) *The Jew's Body*, London, Routledge

Gilman, Sander L. (1999) *Making the Body Beautiful: A Cultural History of Aesthetic Surgery*, Princeton, Princeton University Press

Gilroy, Paul (2004) *After Empire, Melancholia or Convivial Culture?*, London, Routledge

Gilroy, Paul (2005) 'Multiculture, Double Consciousness and the "War on Terror"', *Patterns of Prejudice*, Vol. 39, No. 4

Giroux, Henry (2003) 'Spectacles of Race and Pedagogies of Denial: Anti-Black Racist Pedagogy under the Reign of Neoliberalism', *Communication Education* Vol. 52, No. 3

Glaister, Dan (2006) 'US Officer Guilty of Killing Iraqi General During Questioning', *Guardian*, 23/1/06

Global Policy Forum (2007) 'War and Occupation in Iraq', New York, Global Policy Forum, http://www.global.policy.org/security/issues/iraq/occupation/report/index. htm

Goldberg, David Theo (2002) *The Racial State*, Oxford, Blackwell

Goldstein, Joshua S. (2001) *War and Gender*, Cambridge, Cambridge University Press

Goodey, Jo (2006) 'Ethnic Profiling, Criminal (In)justice and Minority Populations' *Critical Criminology* Vol. 14, No. 3

Gooding-Williams, Robert (1993) *Reading Rodney King: Reading Urban Uprising*, London, Routledge

Gordon, Avery F. (2006) 'Abu Ghraib: Imprisonment and the War on Terror', *Race and Class*, Vol. 48, No. 42

Gordon, Max (2004) 'Abu Ghraib: postcards from the edge', www.opendemocracy. net, 14/10/04

Gottlieb, Julie, V. (2002) '"Motherly Hate": Gendering Anti-Semitism in the British Union of Fascists', *Gender and History*, Vol. 14, No. 2

Gottschalk, Peter (2007) *Islamophobia: Making Muslims the Enemy*, Lanham, MD, Rowman & Littlefield

Gove, Michael (2006) *Celsius 7/7*, London, Weidenfeld & Nicolson

Gow, James (2004) *Defending the West*, Cambridge, Polity

Gray, Herman (1995) 'Black Masculinity and Visual Culture', *Callaloo*, Vol. 18, No. 2

Gray, John (2004) 'Power and Vainglory' in Danner 2004

Green, Penny (1992) 'The Enemy Without: Policing and Class Consciousness in the Miners' Strike', *Journal of Law and Society*, Vol. 19, No. 2

Greenberg, Karen J. (2006) *The Torture Debate in America*, Cambridge, Cambridge University Press

Greene, David L. (2003) 'Bush turns increasingly to language of religion', *Baltimore Sun*, 10/2/03

Grewal, Inderpal (2005) *Transnational America, Feminisms, Diasporas, Neoliberalisms*, Durham, Duke University Press

Grewal, Inderpal; Kaplan, Caren (1994) *Scattered Hegemonies, Postmodernity and Transnational Feminist Practices*, Minneapolis, University of Minnesota Press

Grey, Stephen (2005) 'Torture's Tipping Point', *New Statesman*, London, 19/12/05

Grey, Stephen (2006) *Ghost Plane: The Inside Story of the CIA's Secret Rendition Programme*, London, Hurst & Co

Grosrichard, Alain (1998) *The Sultan's Court: European Fantasies of the East*, London, Verso

Guardian (2005a) 'Torture Evidence Inadmissible in UK Courts, Lords Rules', 8/12/05

Guardian (2005b) 'No record of rendition flights in UK, says Straw', 12/12/05

Gunning, Sandra (1997) *Rape, Race and Lynching*, New York, Oxford University Press

Hables Gray, Chris (1997) *Postmodern War: The New Politics of Conflict*, New York, Guilford Press

Hall, Rachel (2007) 'Of Ziploc Bags and Black Holes: The Aesthetics of Transparency in the War on Terror', *Communication Review*, Vol. 10, No. 4

Hall, Stuart (1997) *Representation: Cultural Representations and Signifying Practices*, London, Sage

Hall, Stuart; Critcher, Charles; Jefferson, Tony; Clarke, John; Robert, Brian (1978) *Policing the Crisis: Mugging, the State and Law and Order*, Houndmills, Basingstoke, Palgrave Macmillan

Hallsworth, S. (2006) 'Racial Targeting and Social Control: Looking Behind the Police', *Critical Criminology*, Vol. 14, No. 3

Hamilton, Carrie (2007) *Women and ETA: The Gender Politics of Radical Basque Nationalism*, Manchester, Manchester University Press

Harbury, Jennifer K. (2005) *Truth, Torture, and the American Way*, Boston, Beacon Press

Harris, John (2005) *So Now Who Do We Vote For?*, London, Faber

Harvey, David (2003) *The New Imperialism*, Oxford, Oxford University Press

Hawkes, G. (2004) *Sex and Pleasure in Western Culture*, Cambridge, Polity

Hedley, Alan (2002) *Running Out of Control: Dilemmas of Globalisation*, Bloomfield, CT, Kumarian

Hendrixson, Anne (2004) 'Angry Young Men, Veiled Young Women: Constructing a New Population Threat', *Corner House Briefing* No. 34, December 2004, Sturminster Newton, Dorset, Corner House

Herold, Marc W. (2002) 'US Bombing and Afghan Civilian Deaths: The Official Neglect of "Unworthy" Bodies', *International Journal of Urban and Regional Research*, Vol. 26, No. 3

Hersh, Seymour (2004a) 'The Gray Zone', *The New Yorker*, 24/5/2004

Hersh, Seymour M. (2004b) *Chain of Command: The Road from 9/11 to Abu Ghraib*, New York, HarperCollins

Herzog, Dagmar (2005) *Sexuality and German Fascism*, Oxford, Berghahn

Hesford, Wendy S.; Kozol, Wendy (2005) *Transnational Feminisms and the Politics of Representation*, New York, Rutgers University Press

Hewitt, Roger (2005) *White Backlash and the Politics of Multiculturalism*, Cambridge, Cambridge University Press

Hirst, Paul (2001) *War and Power in the 21st Century*, Cambridge, Polity

Hjarvard, Stig (2003) *Media in a Globalized Society*, Copenhagen, Museum Tusculanem Press

Ho, Christina (2007) 'Muslim Women's new defenders: women's rights, nationalism and Islamophobia in contemporary Australia', *Women's Studies International Forum*, Vol. 30, No. 4

Hoagland, Jim (2005) 'Pricey Rendition', *Washington Post,* 3/7/05

Home Office (2001) *Community Cohesion: Report of the Independent Review Team*, chaired by Ted Cantle, London, Home Office

hooks, bell (1992) *Black Looks: Race and Representation*, Cambridge, MA, South End Press

hooks, bell (1994) *Outlaw Culture: Resisting Representations*, New York, Routledge

Hudson, Valerie; Den Boer, Andrea (2004) *Bare Branches: The Security Implications of Asia's Surplus Male Population*, Cambridge, MA, MIT Press

Huggins, Martha K. (1991) *Vigilantism and the State in Modern Latin America: Essays on Extra-Legal Violence*, Westport CT, Praeger

Human Rights Watch (2005) *Guantánamo: Detainees' Accounts,* http://www.hrw.org/backgrounder/usa/gitmo1004/index.htm, accessed 23/12/05

Hundal, Sunny (2007) 'The Multicultural Straitjacket', www.opendemocracy.net 20/5/07

Hunt, Krista; Rygiel, Kim (2006) *(En)Gendering the War on Terror*, Aldershot, Ashgate

Hunt, T.; Lessard, M. (2002) *Women and the Colonial Gaze*, New York, New York University Press

Huntington, Nicholas; Bale, Tim (2002) 'New Labour: New Christian Democracy?' *The Political Quarterly*, Vol. 73, No. 1, January

Huntington, Samuel P. (1996) *The Clash of Ciivlizations: Remaking of World Order*, New York, Touchstone

Hurd, Elizabeth S. (2004) 'The Political Authority of Secularism in International Relations', *European Journal of International Relations*, Vol. 10, No. 2

Hurrell, Andrew; Woods, Ngaire (1999) *Inequality, Globalisation and World Politics*, Oxford, Oxford University Press

Ignatieff, M. (2003) *Empire Lite: Nation Building in Bosnia, Kosovo and Afghanistan*, London, Vintage

Ilkkarracan, Pinar (2007) 'Do women and girls have human rights?', www.opendemocracy.net, 26/2/07

Institute of Race Relations (2001) *The Three Faces of British Racism*, London, Institute of Race Relations

International Women's Health Coalition (2004) 'Bush's Other War: The assault on women and girls' sexual and reproductive health and rights', www.iwhc.org

Israely, Jeff (2005) 'Behind the Vatican's Proposed Gay Seminarian Ban', *Time*, 22/9/05

Jackson, Richard (2007) 'Language, Policy and the Construction of a Torture Culture in the War on Terror', *Review of International Studies*, Vol. 33, No. 3

Jackson, Stevi (1999) *Heterosexuality in Question*, London, Sage

Jacobs, Susie; Jacobson, Ruth (2000) *States of Conflict: Gender, Violence and Resistance*, London, Zed

Jacoby, Tami Amanda (2005) *Women in Zones of Conflict, Power and Resistance in Israel, Montreal and London*, McGill-Queen's University Press

Jeffery, Simon; Ryan, Rosalind (2005) 'Prewar claims "sourced from rendition detainee"', *Guardian*, 9/12/05

Johns, Fleur (2005) 'Guantánamo Bay and the Annihilation of the Exception', *European Journal of International Law*, Vol. 16, No. 4

Johnson, Chalmers (2000) *Blowback: The Costs and Consequences of American Empire*, London, Time Warner

Johnson, Marilynn S. (2003) *Street Justice: A History of Police Violence in New York City*, New York, Beacon Press

Jones, A. (2006) *Genocide: A Comprehensive Introduction*, London, Routledge

Kaldor, M. (1999) *New and Old Wars: Organized Violence in a Global Era*, Cambridge, Polity

Kampworth, Karen (2002) *Women and Guerrilla Movements: Nicaragua, El Salvador, Chiapas, Cuba, Pennsylvania*, Penn State University Press

Kaplan, Caren (1994) 'The Politics of Location as Transnational Feminist Critical Practice' in Grewal and Kaplan

Kaplan, E. (2005) *With God on Their Side: George W. Bush and the Christian Right*, New York, New Press

Kapur, Ratna (2002) 'Un-veiling women's rights in the "war on terrorism"', *Duke Journal of Gender Policy and Law*, 2

Kasem, Abul (2003) 'Sex and Sexuality in Islam', www.islam-watch.org

Kellner, Douglas (2003) *From 9/11 to Terror War: The Dangers of the Bush Legacy*, Lanham MD, Rowman & Littlefield

Khalaf, Roula (2005) 'Urgent challenges of Muslim integration in Europe', *Financial Times*, 14/7/05

Khan, Arshad (2003) *Islam, Muslims and America: Understanding the Basis of the Conflict*, New York, Algora Publishing

Khouri, Rami (2004) 'Abu Ghraib in the Arab mirror', www.opendemocracy.com, 19/10/2004

Kiernan, V. G. (1978/2005) *America, The New Imperialism: From White Settlement to World Hegemony*, London, Verso

King, Mike (2006) 'Global Security and Policing Change: The Impact of "Securitisation" on Policing in England and Wales', *Police Practice and Research* Vol. 7, No. 5

Klein, Naomi et al. (2005) *No War: America's Real Business in Iraq*, London, Gibson Square

Knox, Katharine (1999) *Refugees in an Age of Genocide*, London, Routledge

Koch, Richard; Smith, Chris (2006) *Suicide of the West*, London, Continuum

Kontominas, Belinda (2007) 'Gender Imbalance a Threat to Stability', *Sydney Morning Herald*, 31/10/07

Korten, David C. (2001) *When Corporations Rule the World*, San Francisco, Berrett-Koehler

Krishna, Sumi (2007) *Women's Livelihood Rights: Recasting Citizenship for Development*, London, Sage

Krog, Antjie (2000) *Country of My Skull: Guilt, Sorrow and the Limits of Forgiveness in the New South Africa*, New York, Three Rivers Press

Kull, Steven et al. (2004) *Americans on Detention, Torture and the War on Terror*, PIPA/Knowledge Networks Poll, 22/7/04

Kundnani, Arun (2002) 'The Death of Multiculturalism', www.irr.org.uk

Kundnani, Arun (2007) 'Integrationism: The Politics of Anti-Muslim Racism', *Race and Class*, Vol. 48, No. 4

Kuperman, Alan J. (2001) *The Limits of Humanitarian Intervention: Genocide in Rwanda*, Washington DC, Brookings Institution Press

Laqueur, Walter (1996) *Fascism: Past, Present and Future*, Oxford, Oxford University Press

Laqueur, Walter (1999) *The New Terrorism, Fanaticism and the Arms of Mass Destruction*, Oxford, Oxford University Press

Lazreg, Marnia (2007) *Torture and the Twilight of Empire: From Algiers to Baghdad*, Princeton, Princeton University Press

Leach, Robert (2002) 'Historical and Contemporary Significance of Christian Socialism within the Labour Party', http://www.psa.ac.uk/journals/pdf/5/2002/leach.pdf

Leigh, David (2004) 'UK Forces taught torture methods', *Guardian*, 8/5/04

Lentin, R.; Lentin, A. (2006) *Race and State*, Cambridge, Cambridge Scholars Press

Lentin, Ronit (2008) *Thinking Palestine*, London, Zed

Lepard, Brian D. (2002) *Rethinking Humanitarian Intervention*, Pennsylvania, Penn State University Press

Levinson, Sanford (2004) *Torture: A Collection*, Oxford, Oxford University Press

Lewis, Bernard (2004) *The Crisis of Islam, Holy War and Unholy Terror*, London, Phoenix Books

Lewis, Reina (1996) *Gendering Orientalism: Race, Femininity and Representation*, London, Routledge

Lewis, Reina (2004) *Rethinking Orientalism: Women, Travel and the Ottoman Harem*, London, I.B.Tauris

Lincoln, Martha (2007) 'Black Hole, Gulag, Country Club: A Map of Guantánamo Bay', *Socialism and Democracy*, Vol. 21, No. 2

Lis, Jonathan (2007) 'Police Suspect Anti-Gay Protesters Planted Bomb near Fence', www.haaretz.com, 21/9/07

Loader, Ian (2002) 'Policing, Securitization and Democratization in Europe', *Criminology and Criminal Justice* Vol. 2, No. 2

Lovenduski, Joni (2005) *State Feminism and Political Representation*, Cambridge, Cambridge University Press

Luban, David (2006) 'Liberalism, Torture and the Ticking Bomb' in Karen J. Greenberg, *The Torture Debate in America*, Cambridge, Cambridge University Press

MacAskill, Ewen (2005) 'US embassy close to admitting Syria rendition flight', *Guardian*, 27/12/05

MacMaster, Neil (2002) 'The Torture Controversy (1998–2002): Towards a "New History" of the Algerian War?', *Modern and Contemporary France* Vol. 10, No. 4

Macmaster, Neil (2004) 'Torture: from Algiers to Abu Ghraib', *Race and Class*, Vol. 46, No. 1

MacPherson Watt, Steven (2005) 'Torture, "Stress and Duress", and Rendition as Counterterrorism Tools', in Rachel Meeropol (ed.), *America's Disappeared: Secret Imprisonment, Detainees, and the 'War on Terror'*, New York, Seven Stories Press

Mahajan, Rahul (2002) *The New Crusade: America's War on Terrorism*, New York, Monthly Review Press

Mani, Lata (1998) *Contentious Traditions: The Debate about Sati in Colonial India*,

Berkeley, University of California Press

Mann, Michael (2004) *Fascists*, Cambridge, Cambridge University Press

Margulies, Joseph (2007) *Guantánamo and the Abuse of Presidential Power*, New York, Simon and Schuster

Mayer, Jane (2005) 'Outsourcing Torture, the Secret History of America's "Extraordinary Rendition" Program', *New Yorker*, 14/2/05

Mazarr, Michael J. (2007) *Unmodern Men in the Modern World, Radicalism, Terrorism and the War on Modernity*, Cambridge, Cambridge University Press

McCoy, Alfred W. (2006) *A Question of Torture: CIA Interrogation, from the Cold War to the War on Terror*, New York, Metropolitan Books

McKay, George (1998) *DiY Culture: Party and Protest in Nineties' Britain*, London, Verso

McKenzie, John M. (1986) *Propaganda and Empire: Manipulation of British Public Opinion 1880–1960*, Manchester, Manchester University Press

McLintock, Anne (1993) *Imperial Leather: Race, Gender and Sexuality in the Colonial Context*, London and New York, Routledge

McRobbie, Angela (2000) 'Feminism and the Third Way', *Feminist Review*, Vol. 64, No. 1

McRobbie, Angela (2007) 'Top Girl?', *Cultural Studies*, Vol. 21, No. 4

Memmi, Albert (1974) *The Colonizer and the Colonized*, London, Souvenir Press

Mernissi, Fatima (1992) *The Veil and the Male Elite: A Feminist Interpretation of Women's Rights in Islam*, New York, Perseus Books

Mertus, Julie A. (2000) *War's Offensive on Women: The Humanitarian Challenge of Bosnia, Kosovo and Afghanistan*, Bloomfield, Connecticut, Kumarian Press

Metress, Christopher (2002) The Lynching of Emmett Till: A Documentary Narrative, Charlottesville VA, University of Virginia Press

Miles, Robert (1989) *Racism*, London, Routledge

Mills, N.; Brunner, K. (2002) *The New Killing Fields: Massacre and the Politics of Intervention*, New York, Basic Books

Miraj, Ali (2006) 'Muslim anger must be recognised', www.telegraph.co.uk, 13/8/06

Mirza, Heidi Safia (1997) *Black British Feminism: A Reader*, London, Routledge

Mishra, Smeeta (2007) '"Liberation" vs. "Purity": Representations of Saudi Women in the American Press and American Women in the Saudi Press', *Howard Journal of Communications,* Vol. 18, No. 3

Moallem, Minoo (2005) *Between Warrior Brother and Veiled Sister: Islamic Fundamentalism and the Cultural Politics of Patriarchy*, Berkeley, University of California Press

Modood, Tariq (1992) *Not Easy Being British: Colour, Culture and Citizenship*, Stoke-on-Trent, Trentham

Modood, Tariq (2005) 'Remaking Multiculturalism After 7/7', www.opendemocracy.net

Modood, Tariq (2007) *Multiculturalism*, Cambridge, Polity

Modood, Tariq; Triandafyllidou, Anna; Zapata-Barrero, Ricard (2006) *Multiculturalism, Muslims and Citizenship: A European Approach*, London, Routledge

Moghadam, Valentine M. (2005) *Globalizing Women: Transnational Feminist Networks*, Johns Hopkins University Press

Mohanram, Radhika (1999) *Black Body, Women, Colonialism and Space*, St Leonards, NSW, Allen & Unwin

Mohanty, Chandra Talpade (1988) 'Under Western Eyes: Feminist Scholarship and Colonial Discourses', *Feminist Review*, No. 30

Mohanty, Chandra Talpade (2002) '"Under Western Eyes" Revisited: Feminist Solidarity Through Anticapitalist Struggles', *Signs*, Vol. 28, No. 2

Mohanty, Chandra Talpade (2003) *Feminism without Borders*, Durham, Duke University Press

Mohanty, Chandra Talpade (2006) 'US Empire and the Project of Women's Studies: Stories of Citizenship, Complicity and Dissent', *Gender, Place and Culture*, Vol. 13, No. 1, pp. 7–20, February

Monbiot, George (2005) 'How Britain denies its Holocausts', *Guardian*, London, 27/12/05

Money, Jeannette (1999) *Fences and Neighbours: The Political Geography of Immigration Control*, Ithaca, Cornell University Press

Mooers, C. (2006) *The New Imperialists: Ideologies of Empire*, Oxford, Oneworld

Moon, Katharine (1997) *Sex among Allies: Military Prostitution in US-Korea Relations*, New York, Columbia University Press

Moraga, C.; Anzaldua, G. (1983) *This Bridge Called My Back: Writings by Radical Women of Colour*, Boston, Kitchen Table Press

Muaddi Darraj, Susan (2002) 'Understanding the Other Sister: The Case of Arab Feminism', *Monthly Review*, March 2002

Murphy, Ray (2003) 'Guantánamo Bay Detainees', *Human Rights Law Review*, Vol. 3, No. 2

Naber, Nadine (2006) 'Arab-American Femininities: Beyond Arab Virgin/ American-ised Whore', *Feminist Studies* Vol. 32, No. 1

Nagel, Joane (2005) *The Militarization of Race, Gender, and Sexuality in the Iraq War* (with Lindsey Feitz). Annual meeting of the American Sociological Association, Philadelphia, 2005

Nandy, Lisa (2005) 'The Impact of Government Policy on Asylum-seeking and Refugee Children', *Children and Society*, Vol. 19

Nayak, Meghana and Suchland, Jennifer (2006) 'Gender Violence and Hegemonic Projects', *International Feminist Journal of Politics*, Vol. 8, No. 4

Neubeck, Kenneth J.; Cazanave, Noel A. (2001) *Welfare Racism*, Abingdon, Taylor & Francis

Newton, Huey P. (1996) *War Against the Panthers: A Study of Repression in America*, New York, Harlem River Press

Nordstrom, Carolyn (2005) '(Gendered) war', *Studies in Conflict and Terrorism*, 28

Norris, Pippa; Inglehart, Ronald (2002) 'Islamic Culture and Democracy: testing the "Clash of Civilizations" thesis', *Comparative Sociology*, Vol. 1, No. 3–4

Northcott, Michael (2004) *Angel Directs the Storm: Apocalyptic Religion and American Empire*, London, I.B.Tauris

Nussbaum, Martha C. (2000) *Women and Human Development: The Capabilities Approach*, Cambridge, Cambridge University Press

Oates, Lauryn (2006) *Taking Stock Update: Afghan Women and Girls Five Years On*, London, Womankind Worldwide

Okin, Susan Moller (1999) *Is Multiculturalism Bad for Women?* Princeton, NJ, Princeton University Press

Ong, Aihwa (1997) '"A Better Tomorrow"? The Struggle for Global Visibility', *Sojourn*, Vol. 12, No. 2

Oosterhoff, Pauline; Zwanikken, Prisca; Ketting, Evert (2004) 'Sexual Torture of Men in Croatia and Other Conflict Situations: An Open Secret', *Reproductive Health Matters*, 12:23

Otterman, Michael (2007) *American Torture: From the Cold War to Abu Ghraib and Beyond*, London, Pluto

Ouzgane, Lahoucine (2006) *Islamic Masculinities*, London, Zed

Parenti, Christian (2000) *Lockdown America: Police and prisons in the age of crisis*, London, Verso

Parenti, Christian (2003) *The Soft Cage: Surveillance in America from Slavery to the War on Terror*, New York, Basic Books

Patai, Raphael (1973) *The Arab Mind*, New York, Scribner

Peschek, Joseph G. (2005) *The Politics of Empire: War, Terror and Hegemony*, London, Taylor & Francis

Peters, Edward (1985) *Torture*, New York, Basil Blackwell

Pettman, J. J. (1996) *Worlding Women: A Feminist International Politics*, London, Routledge

Philipose, Liz (2007) 'The Politics of Pain and the End of Empire', *International Feminist Journal of Politics*, Vol. 9, No. 1

Phillips, A. (2007) *Multiculturalism without Culture*, Princeton, NJ, Princeton University Press

Phillips, Melanie (2006) *Londonistan, How Britain is Creating a Terror State Within*, London, Gibson Square

Pilger, John (2004) 'Torture is news but it's not new', *Daily Mirror*, London, 7/5/04

Plummer, Ken (1995) *Telling Sexual Stories*, London, Routledge

Pratt, Mary Louise (1992) *Imperial Eyes: Studies in Travel Writing and Transculturation*, London, Routledge

Priest, Dana (2004) 'Jet is an open secret in terror war', *Washington Post*, 27/12/04

Procida, Mary A. (2002) *Married to the Empire: Gender, Politics and Imperialism in India 1883–1947*, Manchester, Manchester University Press

Puar, Jasbir K. (2004) 'Abu Ghraib: Arguing Against Exceptionalism' *Feminist Studies*, Vol. 30 No. 2, Summer

Puar, Jasbir K. (2005a) 'On Torture: Abu Ghraib', *Radical History Review*, No. 93

Puar, Jasbir K. (2005b) 'Queer Times, Queer Assemblages', *Social Text*, Vol. 23, Nos 3–4

Puar, Jasbir K. (2006) 'Mapping US Homonormativities', *Gender, Place and Culture* Vol. 13, No. 1

Puar, Jasbir K.; Rai, Amit S. (2002) 'Monster, terrorist, fag: the War on Terror and the Production of Docile Patriots', *Social Text*, Vol. 20, No. 3, Fall

Puar, Jasbir K.; Rai, Amit S. (2004) 'The Remaking of a Model Minority: Perverse Projectiles under the Specter of (Counter)Terrorism', *Social Text*, Vol. 22, No. 3 Fall

Qureshi, Emran; Sells, Michael Anthony (2003) *The New Crusades: Constructing the Muslim Enemy*, New York, Columbia University Press

Rai, Amit S. (2004) 'Of Monsters: Biopower, Terrorism and Excess in Genealogies of Monstrosity', *Cultural Studies*, Vol. 18, No. 4

Ramadan, T. (2004) *Western Muslims and the Future of Islam*, Oxford, Oxford University Press

Ramsey, Maureen (2006) 'Can the Torture of Terrorist Suspects be Justified?', *International Journal of Human Rights*, Vol. 10, No. 2

Rankin, L. Pauline; Vickers, Jill (2001) 'Women's Movements and State Feminism: Integrating Diversity into Public Policy', Status of Women, Canada, May 2001, http://www.swc-cfc.gc.ca

Rantanan, T. (2005) *The Media and Globalization*, London, Sage

Rao, A. (2001) 'Problems of Violence, States of Terror: Torture in Colonial India', *Interventions: International Journal of Postcolonial Studies*, Vol. 3, No. 2

RAWA (2002) Revolutionary Association of the Women of Afghanistan 'Afghanistan is again the world's largest opium producer, UN', October 25 2002, http://www.rawa.org/opium-again.htm

Rawnsley, Andrew (2000) *Servants of the People*, London, Hamish Hamilton

Reitman, Oonagh (2005) 'Multiculturalism and Feminism: Incompatibility, Compatibility or Synonymity', *Ethnicities*, Vol. 5, No. 2

Reynolds, Paul (2005) 'Blair's "International Community" Doctrine", BBC News 6 March, http://news.bbc.co.uk/71/hi/uk_politics/3539125.stm

Rice, Condoleezza (2005) '"Renditions save lives": Condoleezza Rice's Full Statement', *Times Online*, 5/12/05

Richards, Andrew S. (1997) *Miners on Strike: Class Solidarity and Division in Britain*, Oxford, Berg

Richter-Montpetit, Melanie (2007) 'Empire, Desire and Violence: A Queer Transnational Feminist Reading of the Prisoner "Abuse" in Abu Ghraib and the Question of "Gender Equality"', *International Feminist Journal of Politics*, Vol 9, No. 1

Richters, Juliet (2006) 'Circumcision and the Socially Imagined Sexual Body', *Health Sociology Review*, 15

Ripley, Amanda (2004) 'The rules of interrogation', http://www.time.com, 9/5/04

Rippin, Andrew (2005) *Muslims: Their Religious Beliefs and Practices*, London, Routledge

Rodriguez, Deborah; Ohlson, Kristin (2007) *Kabul Beauty School: An American Woman Goes Behind the Veil*, New York, Random House

Rotberg, Robert I. (2003) *State Failure and State Weakness in a Time of Terror*, Washington DC, Brookings Institution Press

Roth, Kenneth, Worden, Minky (eds) (2005) *Torture, Does it Make Us Safer? Is It Ever OK? A Human Rights Perspective*, New York, New Press

Rowe, Michael (2004), *Policing, Race and Racism*, Cullompton, Devon, Willan Publishing

Rubin, Gayle (1975) 'The Traffic in Women: Notes on the Political Economy of Sex', in Rayna R. Reiter (ed.), *Toward an Anthropology of Women*, New York, Monthly Review Press

Russell, Meg (2005) *The Building of New Labour: The Politics of a Party Organsiation*, Basingstoke, Palgrave

Saggar, Shamit (2003) 'Immigration and the Politics of Public Opinion', *Political Quarterly*, October 2003, Vol. 74, No. 4

Said, E. (1979) *Orientalism*, London, Vintage

Said, Edward (2003) 'Orientalism 25 Years Later: Worldly Humanism v. the Empire-Builders', www.counterpunch.org, 4/8/03

Sands, Phillipe (2005) *Lawless World*, London, Penguin

Sanoff, Alvin P. (2005) 'Unveiling Islam', The Washingtonian, 1/1/05

Sawday, Jonathan (1995) *The Body Emblazoned, Dissection and the Human Body in Renaissance Culture*, London, Routledge

Scarry, Elaine (1985) *The Body in Pain: The Making and Unmaking of the World*, Oxford, Oxford University Press

Scherer, M.; Benjamin, M. (2003) 'The Abu Ghraib Files', www.salon.com, October

Schiessl, Christoph (2002) 'An Element of Genocide: Rape, Total War, and International Law in the Twentieth Century', *Journal of Genocide Research*, June 2002, Vol. 4, No. 2

Schmidt, Catherine; Joffe, George; Davar, Elisha (2005) 'The Psychology of Political Extremism', *Cambridge Review of International Affairs*, Vol. 18, No. 1

Scott, Joan (2005) 'Symptomatic Politics, the Banning of Islamic Headscarves in French Public Schools', *French Politics, Culture and Society*, Vol. 23, No. 3 Winter

Scraton, Phil (2002) *Beyond September 11, An Anthology of Dissent*, London, Pluto

Seaton, Matt (2002) 'My son the fanatic. Are the parents to blame when a child of the west turns Islamist extremist?' *Guardian*, 2/1/02

Segal, Lynne (1994) *Straight Sex: Rethinking the Politics of Pleasure*, London, Virago

Sengupta, Kim (2008) 'Sentenced to Death: Afghan who dared to read about women's rights', *Independent*, 31/1/08

Sedou Herr, Ranjoo (2003) 'The Possibility of Nationalist Feminism', *Hypatia*, Vol. 18, No. 13, Fall

Shaaban, Thaina (1993) 'The Hidden History of Arab Feminism', *Ms*, May/June

Sharifzada, Mohammad Jawad (2006) 'Slow Progress on Women's Rights', London, Institute for War and Peace Reporting

Shaw, Robert (2003) *The Epidemic: The Rot of American Culture, Absentee and Permissive Parenting*, New York, HarperCollins

Shawcross, W. (2000) *Deliver Us from Evil: Warlords and Peacekeepers in a World of Endless Conflict*, London, Bloomsbury Press

Shepherd, Laura J. (2006) 'Veiled References: Constructions of gender in the Bush Administration Discourse on the Attacks on Afghanistan Post-9/11', *International Feminist Journal of Politics*, Vol. 8, No. 1

Shore, Zachary (2006) *Breeding Bin Ladens: America, Islam and the Future of Europe*, Baltimore, Johns Hopkins University Press

Silverman, Jon (2005) 'Torture Ruling's International Impact', www.news.bbc.co.uk, 8/12/05

Sjoberg, Laura (2007) 'Agency, Militarized Femininity and Enemy Others: Observations From The War In Iraq', *International Feminist Journal of Politics*, Vol. 9, No. 1

Sloterdijk, Peter (1988) *Critique of Cynical Reason*, London, Verso

Solomos, John; Back, Les (1996) *Racism and Society*, London, Macmillan

Solomos, J.; Murji, K. (2005) *Racialization: Studies in Theory and Practice*, Oxford, Oxford University Press

Sontag, S. (2004) 'Regarding the Torture of Others', *New York Times*, 23 May

Sorensen, Lita (2003) *The Scotsboro Boys Trial: A Primary Source Account*, New York, Rosen Publishing Group

Soros, George (2004) *The Bubble of American Supremacy*, London, Phoenix

Spackman, Barbara (1996) *Fascist Virilities: Rhetoric, Ideology, and Social Fantasy in Italy*, Minneapolis, University of Minnesota Press

Spillers, Hortense (1987) 'Mama's Baby, Papa's Maybe: An American Grammar Book', *Diacritics*, Summer

Spivak, Gayatri Chakravorty (1987) *In Other Worlds: Essays in Cultural Politics*, New York, Methuen

Spivak, Gayatri Chakravorty (1988) 'Can the Subaltern Speak?' in C. Nelson and L. Grossberg, *Marxism and the Interpretation of Culture*, Basingstoke, Macmillan

Sreberny-Mohammadi, Annabelle; Winseck, Dwayne; McKenna, Jim; Boyd-Barrett, Oliver (1997) *Media in Global Context: A Reader*, London, Hodder Arnold

Stabile, C.; Kumar, D. (2005) 'Unveiling Imperialism: Media, Gender and the War on Afghanistan', *Media, Culture and Society*, Vol. 27, No. 5

Stafford Smith, Clive (2005) 'Inside Guantánamo', *New Statesman*, London, 21/11/05

Stafford Smith, Clive (2007) *Bad Men, Guantánamo Bay and the Secret Prisons*, London, Weidenfeld & Nicolson

Stam, Juan (2003) 'Bush's Religious Language', *The Nation*, 22/12/03

Stanford Friedman, Susan (2001) 'Feminism, State Fictions and Violence: Gender, Geopolitics and Transnationalism' *Communal/Plural*, Vol. 9, No. 1

Steans, Jill (2008) 'Telling Stories about Women and Gender in the War on Terror', *Global Society* Vol. 22, No. 1

Stephens, Otis H. (2004) 'Presidential Power, Judicial Deference, and the Status of Detainees in an Age of Terrorism' in David B. Cohen and John W. Wells (eds), *American National Security and Civil Liberties in an Era of Terrorism*. Basingstoke, Palgrave Macmillan

Steyn, Johan (2004) 'Guantánamo Bay: The Legal Black Hole', *International and Comparative Law Quarterly*, Vol. 53, No. 1

Stiglmayer, Alexandra (1994) *Mass Rape: the War against Women in Bosnia-Herzegovina*, Lincoln, University of Nebraska Press

Stoler, Ann Laura (1995) *Race and the Education of Desire*, Durham, Duke University Press

Stonor Saunders, Frances (1999) *Who Paid the Piper? the CIA and the Cultural Cold War*, London, Granta

Strasser, Steven (2004) *The Abu Ghraib Investigations: The Official Independent Panel and Pentagon Reports on the Shocking Prisoner Abuse in Iraq*, New York, Public Affairs

Taguba, A. (2004) Investigation of the 800th Military Police Brigade known as 'Th Taguba Report', http://www.dod.gov/pubs/foi/detainees/taguba/

Tatchell, P. (2005) '2000 years of Church homophobia', http://www.petertatchell.net/religion/2000.htm

Taylor, Gary; Spencer, Steve (2004) *Social Identities: Multidisciplinary Approaches*, London, Routledge

Taylor, Max; Horgan, John (2006) 'A Conceptual Framework for Addressing Psychological Process in the Development of the Terrorist', *Terrorism and Political Violence*, Vol. 18, No. 4

Theweleit, Klaus (1989) *Male Fantasies*, Vol. 2, Cambridge, Polity

Thobani, Sunera (2007) 'White Wars, Western Feminisms and the "War on Terror"', *Feminist Theory*, Vol. 8, No. 2

Thom, Deborah (2000) *Nice Girls and Rude Girls: Women Workers in World War I*, London, I.B.Tauris

Thomas, Elaine R. (2006) 'Keeping Identity at a Distance: Explaining France's New Legal Restrictions on the Islamic Headscarf', *Ethnic and Racial Studies*, Vol. 29, No. 2

Thomas, Gill (1989) *Life on All Fronts: Women in the First World War*, Cambridge, Cambridge University Press

Thrift, N. (2005) *Knowing Capitalism*, London, Sage

Tiggemann, Marika; Verri, Annapia; Scaravaggi, Sabrina (2005) 'Body Dissatisfaction, Disordered Eating, Fashion Magazines, and Clothes: a cross-cultural comparison between Australian and Italian young women', *International Journal of Psychology*, Vol. 40, No. 5

Travis, Alan; Dyer, Clare; White, Michael (2005) 'Britain "sliding into a police state"', *Guardian*, 28/1/05

UK, *Hansard Parliamentary Debates*, 5th ser., various dates

UK, Department for Communities and Local Govenment, 2008, *Empowering Muslim Women*, 23 January, http://www.communities-gov.uk/news/corporate/ 672344

UNODC (2007) 'Afghanistan, Opium Winter Rapid Assessment Survey', February 2007 http://www.unodc.org/pdf/research/2007_ORAS.pdf

Vallely, Paul (2004) 'A systematic process learned from Cold War', *Independent*, 14/5/04

Waddington, P.A.J. (1999) *Policing Citizens: Authority and Rights*, London, Routledge

Walker, Martin (2006) 'The Geopolitics of Sexual Frustration', paper published by the

Carnegie Endowment for International Peace, Washington DC

Wallace, Michele (2004) *Dark Designs and Visual Culture*, Durham, Duke University Press

Walzer, Michael (1995) *Towards a Global Civil Society*, Oxford, Berghahn

Ware, Vron (1992) *Beyond the Pale, White Women, Racism and History*, London, Verso

Ware, Vron (2007) *Who Cares about Britishness? A Global View of the National Identity Debate*, London, Arcadia

Washington Post (2004) 'Sworn Statements by Abu Ghraib Detainees', http://www.washingtonpost.com/wp-srv/world/iraq/abughraib/swornstatements042104.html, accessed 15/12/05

Watson, Roland (2005) 'US admits guard soiled Koran at Guantanamo', *Times*, 4/6/05

Websdale, N. (2001) *Policing the Poor: From Slave Plantation to Public Housing*, Boston, Northeastern University Press

Weeks, Jeffrey (1985) *Sexuality and Its Discontents: Meanings, Myths and Modern Sexualities*, London, Routledge

Welch, Michael (2002) *Detained: Immigration Laws and the Expanding INS Jail Complex*, Philadelphia, Temple University Press

Went, Robert (2000) *Globalization: Neoliberal Challenge, Radical Responses*, London, Pluto

West, Lois (1997) *Feminist Nationalisms*, London, Routledge

Whitaker, Beth Elise (2007) 'Exporting the Patriot Act? Democracy and the "War on terror" in the Third World', *Third World Quarterly*, Vol. 28, No. 5

Whitlock, Gillian (2000) *The Intimate Empire: Reading Women's Autobiography*, London, Continuum

Wilford, Rick; Miller, Robert L. (1998) *Women, Ethnicity and Nationalism: The Politics of Transition*, London, Routledge

Williams, Mari A. (2002) *A Forgotten Army: The Female Munitions Workers of South Wales, 1939–1945*, Cardiff, University of Wales Press

Winant, Howard (2001) *The World Is a Ghetto: Race and Democracy since World War II*, New York, Basic Books

Winant, Howard (2004) *New Politics of Race: Globalism, Difference, Justice*, Minneapolis, University of Minnesota Press

Winant, Howard (2006) 'Race and Racism; Towards a Global Future', *Ethnic and Racial Studies*, Vol. 29, No. 5, September

Winter, Bronwyn (2006) 'Secularism Aboard the Titanic: Feminism and the Debate over the Hijab in France', *Feminist Studies*, Vol. 32, No. 2

Women and Work Commission (2006) *Shaping a Fairer Future*, London, Department of Trade and Industry

Women's Edge (2007) 'How women in Lesotho got the right to own property', http://www.womensedge.org

Womenwatch (2007) http://www.un.org/womenwatch

Wong, Kam C. (2007) *The Impact of USA PATRIOT Act on American Society: An Evidence-Based Assessment*, Hauppauge, NY, Nova Science Publishers

Woodward, Will (2006) 'Radical Muslims must integrate, says Blair', *Guardian*, 9/12/06

Yee, James (2005) *Guantánamo: The War on Human Rights*, New York, New Press

Yegenoglu, Meyda (1998) *Colonial Fantasies: Towards a feminist reading of Orientalism*, Cambridge, Cambridge University Press

Yotopoulos, Alice; Benedek, Wolfgang (2004) *Anti-Terrorist Measures and Human Rights*, Leiden, Brill, Marangopoulos Foundation for Human Rights, European

Training and Research Centre for Human Rights and Democracy

Young, Iris Marion (1990) *Justice and the Politics of Difference,* Princeton, Princeton University Press

Youngs, Gillian (2000) *Political Economy, Power and the Body*, Houndmills, Basingstoke, Macmillan

Youngs, Gillian (2006) 'Feminist International Relations in the Age of the War on Terror: Ideologies, Religions and Conflict', *International Feminist Journal of Politics*, Vol. 8, No. 1

Yuval-Davis, Nira (1997) *Gender and Nation*, London, Sage

Yuval-Davis, Nira; Anthias, Floya (1989) *Women-Nation-State*, Houndmills, Basingstoke, Macmillan

Zeeland, Steven (1995) *Sailors and Sexual Identity: Crossing the Line between 'Straight' and 'Gay' in the US Navy*, Binghampton, NY, Haworth Press

Zine, Jasmin (2004) 'Staying on the Straight Path: A Critical Ethnography of Islamic Schooling in Ontario', PhD thesis, Department of Sociology and Equity Studies in Education, University of Toronto

Zine, Jasmin (2006) 'Between Orientalism and Fundamentalism: Muslim Women and Feminist Engagement', in Hunt and Rygiel 2006

Žižek, Slavoj (2002) *Welcome to the Desert of the Real*, London, Verso

Žižek, Slavoj (2004) 'Between Two Deaths: The Culture of Torture', *London Review of Books*, 3/6/04

Index